Inception Of

The

Golden Age

A Scientific Discovery

By

Seymour Lessans

ISBN: 978-1-954284-05-0 (Epub)
ISBN: 978-1-954284-13-5 (Paperback)
ISBN: 978-1-954284-16-6 (Adobe PDF)
Safeworld Publishing Company

FOR THE BETTERMENT OF HUMANKIND

TABLE OF CONTENTS

PREFACE

The primary purpose of this book is to reveal a fantastic, scientific discovery about the nature of man whose life, as a direct consequence of this mathematical revelation, will be completely revolutionized in every way for his benefit, bringing about the long-awaited Golden Age prophesied in the Bible.

However, it is necessary that you read this book in its entirety, chapter by chapter, in order to understand it because each part is mathematically related to the whole, which presents a solution to every problem of human conduct. Furthermore, so as to preclude your jumping to conclusions, this book has nothing whatever to do with communism, socialism, capitalism, government, religion, or philosophy; only with the removal of beliefs among the top echelon of your educated who have been unconsciously passing along from generation to generation the most profound ignorance in the guise of genuine knowledge, for which they cannot be blamed.

But because this book dares to oppose the three forces that control the thinking of mankind — Government, Religion, and Education (the most dangerous thinking of all, the kind that really doesn't know the truth, as Socrates observed, but because of some fallacious standard only think they know; the kind of thinking that is responsible for the slaughter of six million Jews, for mental illness, for all wars, prejudice, hate, unemployment, poverty, etc.), I have found it necessary to resort to this manner of introducing my work in the fervent hope that I may break through this sound barrier of learned ignorance and reach the intelligent, thinking portion of mankind before an atomic explosion destroys millions of lives.

It is not necessary to jump to conclusions as ignorance is wont to do because the facts in the book are absolutely undeniable, provided you are not blinded by this mathematical revelation as you come out of Plato's cave, where you have lived so many years in the shadows that distorted your beliefs into a semblance of reality. Remember, your opinion that Earth was flat never altered the truth that it was always round, which discovery did not require your approval for its validity, although your understanding was necessary for recognition and development.

THE AUTHOR

Seymour Lessans passed away in 1991 at the age of 72. This book was his 2nd attempt (7 in all) to demonstrate a scientific discovery regarding the nature of man which has the power to prevent what no one wants: war, crime, discrimination, poverty, and many other evils plaguing mankind. Although some examples in this edition are outdated (this book was first written in 1962) — and certain other changes were made to the economic system in his later writings — the core of his discovery remains sound. It is our hope that you will contain your skepticism long enough to learn what this is all about.

INTRODUCTION

Shortly after my arrival from Mars (I'm sure this sounds strange to your ears, especially with all the science fiction stories available), I was so completely taken aback by the terrible hurt and general unhappiness that prevails among your relations with each other that at first I couldn't believe my eyes, until the reason for this was made apparent by the realization that your scientists in the field of psychology had not yet discovered the mathematical law of man's nature, which, many years ago, brought about on our globe what we refer to as the Great Transition. We have no war, no crime, absolutely nothing that hurts another individual, and what is much more important — no weapons or threat of punishment to control what no one can possibly desire to do.

However, the only reason you have not made this discovery before now is because life began on our planet long before it did on yours, and as a consequence our mental development is far superior. You still play chess, which is an obsolete game on Mars because the person who moves first must lose, and our children in the elementary grades, to draw up a comparison, work on this kind of a problem: They are given 105 alphabetical squares divided equally between A and O, and are told to arrange these in groups of 3 so that each of the identical 15 letters on a line is never twice with the same letter in all 35 groups. When first arriving here, and to test the thinking ability of what you refer to as your intelligentsia, I gave this problem to 10 professors. Eight gave up in despair after working on it for two weeks, and the other two revealed by their answer that they never even understood the problem.

My purpose in making you conscious of this great difference between us is to prepare you for knowledge so fantastic that if it were not mathematically undeniable, the utter confusion of your mind would reject what you cannot understand and yet have been taught through natural ignorance to believe. Truth on your planet is judged not by any mathematical standard, because you have none yet, but by who said what. If your doctor, priest, professor, etc., tells you that something is true or right, you believe him because you have no way of knowing that his knowledge may be false, and he is compelled to justify the truth of his knowledge in order to have you support his manner of earning a living; consequently, he really believes that he knows although in reality he only thinks he knows, as your philosopher Socrates observed. However, this is not a criticism because no one is to blame for what came about out of necessity.

But since I know the solution to your problem, for it is something with which everyone on Mars is familiar, I shall submit this book for the express purpose of revealing a most amazing law which will demonstrate, in a manner your scientists will not be able to deny, not only that the mankind system is just as harmonious as the solar system despite all the evil and ignorance that ever existed, but that the inception of your Golden Age cannot commence until the knowledge pertaining to this law is accurately understood.

Consequently, I shall set sail on a voyage that will perform a virtual miracle by igniting a chain reaction of thought which will explode across your planet and destroy, with its fallout, every possibility of hurt that exists among your relations with each other. So put on your thinking caps and try to deny the mathematical relations soon to be revealed which permit you to foresee this miracle. While God is proven to be a mathematical reality as a consequence of your becoming conscious of the truth, all religion is compelled to take leave of your planet; while crime and war are wiped from the face of Earth, never to return, so likewise are all forms of government, unions, and authority in general; and while your moral code, your Ten Commandments, your standards of right and wrong are completely extirpated, all premarital relations, adultery and divorce will become relics of the past without hurting one single individual and of your own free will. Where did you ever hear anything so fantastic or paradoxical? Is it possible for you to believe it? And aren't you jumping to the conclusion that this is against all human nature?

But shouldn't this news make those individuals who have been trying to correct the evil in the world very happy? If the cry of the clergy is "Faith in God," they should be simply thrilled at the miracle he is about to perform, which reveals his reality, even though it means putting them out of work. If the communist and capitalist governments are truly interested in the welfare of their people, then just imagine how excited they will be to learn that the most perfect relations between man and man will soon be developed, even though it makes their services unnecessary. If a writer is just about ready to submit his book to the public for the express purpose of revealing knowledge on how to raise children or live together in greater harmony as man and wife, he will be absolutely in ecstasy to learn that God is going to bring about such perfect harmony in a short time that all books purporting to do this very thing won't have any more value. Just imagine how happy the profession of psychiatry will be to learn that all its patients will be healed overnight by this miracle, making this service a thing of the past. There is a good deal of humor to this Great Transition which we experienced many years ago, for it reveals how completely dishonest you were compelled to be with yourselves and each other. The only difference between a salesman selling books and a doctor, theologian, etc., is that the former must convince only his prospects, while the latter must also convince himself. The former doesn't care if no one ever reads his books, just so he is paid a commission. The latter is compelled to justify that he knows what he is advising and treating, otherwise he could never accept a fee, gratuity or income for his service. A man who struggles to earn a living doesn't need the same kind of justification, and he will even steal with a clear conscience; but those who have found a certain amount of security in what a part of the world criticizes, are compelled to convince themselves that these others don't know what they're talking about. However, everything was necessary. Now it is time to draw an infallible line of demarcation between what is true and what is false, and you are going to be simply amazed at how much of what is false passed for what is true. But before I begin, let me make certain that I am welcome. Do you want war or peace, unhappiness or happiness, insecurity or security, sickness or health? Do you prefer losing the one you have fallen in love with, or winning and living happily ever after? Do you like when your husband or wife, whom you love, commits adultery and then leaves you for another? If any people on this planet can actually prefer for themselves what they do not want, then I shall be only too glad to return. Since this is a mathematical impossibility because I know that happiness is preferable to unhappiness, health to sickness, etc., I shall now begin a revelation of knowledge which no one will be able to deny — providing the relations are understood. But remember, because a chimpanzee doesn't understand that 3 is to 6 what 4 is to 8 does not negate the validity of this simple equation. Consequently, any truth that is revealed in a mathematical manner does not require your approval, although it does necessitate your understanding and recognition. However, if you are afraid of the truth because it disturbs you to discover how wrong you have been in your opinion of what is right, then I suggest you read another book, since what follows is not meant for your ears.

PART ONE

The Foundation and Development of A Mathematical Standard

CHAPTER 1 — Words, Not Reality

Your problem of hurting each other is very deep-rooted and begins with words through which you have not been allowed to see reality for what it really is. Consequently, your expression — "Sticks and stones will break your bones, but names will never hurt you" is completely fallacious because you have been unconsciously hurt. This unconsciousness has its source in your failure to understand how the eyes function, which is revealed by the fact that you still include them as one of the five senses.

The word sense is defined in general as — "Any of certain agencies by or through which an individual receives impressions of the external world; popularly, one of the five senses. Any receptor, or group of receptors, specialized to receive and transmit external stimuli, as of sight, taste, smell, etc." But this is a wholly fallacious observation because nothing from the external world strikes the optic nerve as stimuli do upon the organs of hearing, taste, touch and smell. An apple, pear, orange, peach and telescope could not be called five fruits obviously because one does not belong in this category.

It can easily be demonstrated at the birth of a child that the eyes are not a sense organ when it can be seen that no object is capable of getting a reaction from the wide-open eyes because absolutely nothing is impinging on the optic nerve, although any number of sounds, tastes, touches or smells can get a reaction. Furthermore, and quite revealing, if this child, immediately after birth, was placed in a soundproof room with the eyelids removed and kept alive for 50 years or longer on a steady flow of intravenous glucose without allowing any stimuli to strike the four organs of sense, this baby, child, young and old man would never be able to see any objects existing in that room no matter how much in motion or colorful they might be, because there is absolutely nothing that travels from an object to the optic nerve that causes sight.

If a lion roared in that room, the child would hear the sound because this impinges on the eardrum and is then transmitted to the brain, and the same holds true for anything that makes direct contact with the body; but this is far from the case with the eyes. Consequently, to call them a sense organ when this describes stimuli from the outside world making contact with a nerve ending, is completely erroneous.

Sight takes place for the first time when the repetition of sense experience makes the child aware that something will soon follow something else, which then arouses attention, anticipation, and a desire to see the objects of the relation. This desire is an electric current that turns on or focuses the eyes to see that which exists, completely independent of man's perception, in the external world. He doesn't see these objects because they strike the optic nerve; he sees them because they are there to be seen. But in order to look, there must be a desire to see. Consequently, if a child was placed in surroundings that eliminate the possibility of sense experience, even though the eyelids were permanently removed, this baby could never desire to see, which is a prerequisite of sight.

The brain is like a very complicated tape recorder, projector, movie camera all rolled into one. As sense experiences become related or recorded, they are projected, through the eyes, upon the screen of the objects held in relation and photographed by the brain. Consequently, everything in the external world is distorted if the words through which man looks at what he calls reality are inaccurate symbols, or if the relation which is photographed becomes, as in "five senses," an inaccurate negative which is then projected realistically upon undeniable substance. The brain photographs all relations, whether true or false, but believing that the eyes are a sense organ unconsciously confirmed what man saw with them because he was unaware that it was possible to project a fallacious relation realistically. To understand this better, let us observe a baby learning his first word.

As his gaze is fixed on a dog, let us repeat rapidly in his ear the word "dog," stopping when his eyes wander. Soon, this relation is formed, which makes him conscious of a particular difference that exists in the external world. As he learns more and more words, such as cat, horse, bird, sun, moon, etc., he becomes conscious of these differences which no one can deny because they are seen through words or slides that circumscribe accurately these various bits of substance. But in the course of development, he learns other kinds of words that form inaccurate relations, and when this happens, he doesn't see a true picture of reality.

The word "beautiful," for example, has no external reality, and yet, because it is learned in association with a particular physiognomy, a beautiful girl is created when no such person exists. There is obviously a difference between the shape and features of individuals, but to label one beautiful and another ugly only reveals that you are conscious of a fallacious difference that is projected through your eyes upon substance that cannot be denied. If a young child, while looking at one type individual, heard over and over again "Look how beautiful!" with the proper inflection, it wouldn't take long before this child would desire to associate with the one type while avoiding the other, and as he would get older you wouldn't be able to convince him that an ugly or beautiful person does not exist as a definite part of the real world.

As a consequence of this belief that one person is more beautiful or handsome than another, which places a greater value on certain features, many people have nose operations while others squeeze their teeth together in an effort to attract someone whom they feel has more to offer, and the doctor, who must earn a living, justifies his professional advice on the undeniable grounds that they will definitely be more attractive when their teeth are together and their nose straightened.

As a further consequence of these fallacious differences that do not exist, but are only a projection of deceptive relations, you have been led to believe that you are more important than someone else, more valuable in the scheme of things, and from this source a host of evils stem. However, it is mathematically impossible to expect you to give up what is also a source of satisfaction, but the change does not depend on those who are happy in their pride and self-importance, which includes everyone to a degree, but on those who are seriously hurt and who are shown how they, too, can become happy.

It is absolutely true that just as long as others consider you more beautiful when you look a certain way, or more educated and intelligent when you do certain things, there is ample justification to change, but what would happen if you lived in an atmosphere where there were no fallacious values? Supposing your ugliest and stupidest girl was placed on our planet, there would be absolutely nothing to prevent her from living a normal life because none of our males would judge her in terms of ugliness or stupidity, for no such thing exists except as a projection of your realistic imagination. But on Earth this girl is handicapped from the day of her birth, not only because she has an aquiline or straight nose, her teeth are apart or together, but because she may be a Jew, Catholic, Protestant, Black, Japanese, German, etc. She is constantly judged not in any direct manner but in a way you cannot correct because you see her through a kaleidoscope of words that transform her realistically into what she is not. Every other word you use stratifies external differences, which cannot be denied, into fallacious values that appear realistic because they are seen with your eyes.

Although you look back with smiling incredulity to the days of yore and wonder about the many ignorant beliefs that your ancestors used to imagine were true, is it impossible for your professors to believe that they are not one whit more educated or intelligent than anybody else? Have they any conception that these are only words? Didn't I look at the people on your planet with smiling incredulity until I realized the true source of your problem? In reality, no one is more intelligent or educated than anyone else, as you will see, but we on our planet appear to be because all the ignorance has been removed and we know ourselves at last for what we really are. You earthlings do not know yourselves and are consciously unconscious of your reason for doing things because of words, nothing else. Your psychologists, theologians, philosophers, as well as all others who read books but don't know the difference between mathematical and logical relations, think that by learning a lot of words in various combinations, they have been studying reality. These people came into existence not because they knew the truth, but only because ignorance was pleading for help and willing to pay for it. Man will pay anything if he believes you can help him, and you, knowing this, will do anything to get him to believe that you can. You are going to get a lot of laughs in this book, but at nobody's expense.

Now two words that you believe are true, just as you did with "five senses," but which are absolutely and positively false, are Free Will. However, the problem here is so deep and so involved that even those like your philosopher Spinoza, who understood that man's will is not free, didn't even come close to the solution, and others like your William James and Will Durant would be willing to bet their life that will is free. I shall illustrate how confused your thinkers are by making a few mathematical observations, those which cannot be denied.

First, it is obvious that man's will is or is not free, just as it is undeniable that God is or is not a reality. Consequently, if it can be demonstrated that it is mathematically impossible to prove free will true, it is also mathematically impossible to prove determinism, as the opposite of free will, false, and this can be done very simply.

To prove this just ask yourself: "Is it possible for any person not to do what he has just done?" Impossible, correct? This is a mathematical relation which is undeniable and is equivalent to asking is it possible for anyone not to get four as an answer to two plus two. Now if what has just been done was the choosing of B instead of A, is it possible not to choose B which has already been chosen? Since it is absolutely impossible not to choose B instead of A once B is selected, how is it possible to choose A in this comparison of possibilities once A has not been preferred, when only one of them can be chosen at that single moment of time? Yet free will, in order to prove itself true, must do just that, the impossible. It must go back, reverse the order of time, undo what has been done, and then show that A could have been chosen instead of B. Is it any wonder free will is still a theory? The great humor in this particular instance lies in the fact that though it was always possible to prove determinism true, theology considered it as absolutely false while dogmatically promulgating, in obedience to God's will, that free will an absolute reality.

Since it is absolutely impossible for free will to ever be proven true (I take for granted this is now understood), nothing in this universe can prove determinism an unreality (and in this context it shall only mean the opposite of free will as death is the opposite of life), simply because this would automatically prove the truth of free will which has been shown to be an impossibility. Consequently, the belief in free will and all conceptions regarding it can only remain in existence as a plausible theory just as long as no undeniable evidence is produced in contravention. Yet to show you how confused the mind can get when mathematical relations are not perceived, your philosopher Will Durant does not agree with this obvious fact because he offers a different reason as to why the belief in free will continues to exist. He writes: "If there is an almost eternal recurrence of philosophies of freedom" (free will) "it is because direct perception can never be beaten down with formulas, or sensation with reasoning." Can you not see how mathematically impossible are his observations? If free will was proven, once and for all, to be that which is nonexistent (and remember this is a possibility only because the reverse is impossible), and accepted as such by your world at large because the proof cannot be denied by anyone anywhere, would it be possible — think about this carefully — for philosophies of freedom to recur anymore? Isn't it obvious that the recurrence of this philosophy is a mathematical impossibility once freedom of the will is proven to be a figment of the imagination, or to phrase it differently, a realistic mirage? Consequently, its continued return can only be due to the fact it is still a theory or plausible conception that has never been dethroned, allowing the belief and its philosophies to persist. But Durant states that philosophies of freedom eternally recur not because of this, which cannot be denied by the common sense of anyone anywhere, even by this philosopher himself once it is pointed out, but "because direct perception can never be beaten down with formulas, or sensation with reasoning." Isn't it apparent to you now that such words have no relation to reality whatever? If this is an example of what he calls direct perception and he considers it superior to reasoning, is it any wonder he is so confused and his reasoning so fallacious since the word because, which denotes the perception of a relation, indicates that he is criticizing reasoning while reasoning. This simple paraphrase will clarify a point: "If there is an almost eternal recurrence of" four equaling two plus two, "it is because" two equals one plus one, and one plus one plus one plus one totals four. He unconsciously uses syllogistic reasoning, which is logical though completely fallacious, by setting up an understandable assumption for a major premise. But when a person perceives certain undeniable relations, is it necessary to make an equation out of four equaling two plus two, or out of the fact that once free will is proven untrue, it can no longer exist and its philosophies of freedom return? Durant begins with the assumption that direct perception, which are words that symbolize what he cannot possibly understand, is superior to reasoning in understanding the truth which made a syllogistic equation necessary to prove the validity of an inaccurate perception. Then he reasons thus in his minor premise: Free will is not a matter of reasoning like determinism, but is the result of direct perception, therefore — and here is his fallacious conclusion — "since

9

philosophies of freedom employ direct perception which can never be beaten down by the reasoning of determinism, the belief in free will must eternally recur." You earthlings have no conception yet of how distorted your words, in various logical combinations, have made your world.

However, the really important factor is not that man's will is not free, but what does this knowledge reveal when sucked dry of its meaning. Your discussions of whether man's will is or is not free, whether God is or is not a reality, are equivalent to the discussions as to what came first, the chicken or the egg; but you were not supposed to know the truth until after the discovery of atomic energy. Consequently, since the real importance lies in the meaning of will not being free, it really doesn't make any difference whether proof is established beforehand because undeniable proof is established in the meaning; but despite this it is still of value to know why man's will is not free, so to familiarize you with mathematical reasoning before we attack the heart of the problem I shall demonstrate in an undeniable manner exactly why will is not free.

Now the dictionary states that free will is "The power of self-determination regarded as a special faculty of choosing good or evil without compulsion or necessity. Made, done, or given of one's own free choice; voluntary." But this is only part of the definition since it is implied that man can be held responsible and blamed for doing what he does. In other words, it is believed that man has the ability to do other than he does — if he wants to — and therefore can be held responsible for doing what he is not supposed to do. These very words reveal the fallacy of this belief to those who have mathematical perception: Man is held responsible not for doing what he desires to do or considers right, better, or good for himself under his particular set of circumstances, but for doing what others judge to be wrong or evil, and they feel absolutely certain he could have acted otherwise had he wanted to. Isn't this the theme of free will? But take note, supposing the alternative judged right for him by others is not desired by himself, what then? Does this make his will free? Can't you see the humor here?

Supposing a father is desperately in need of work to feed his family but can't find a job. Let us assume he is living in the United States and for various reasons doesn't come under the consideration of unemployment compensation or relief, and can't get any more credit for food, clothing, shelter, etc.; what is he supposed to do? If he steals a loaf of bread to feed his family, the law can easily punish him by saying he didn't have to steal if he didn't want to, which is perfectly true. Others might say stealing is *evil*, that he could have chosen *good* which, in this case, was almost any other alternative. But supposing this individual preferred stealing because he considered this act good for himself in comparison to the evil of asking for charity or further credit, does this make his will free? It is obvious that he did not have to steal if he didn't want to, but he wanted to, and it is also obvious that the laws did not have to punish him if they didn't want to, but both sides wanted to do what they did under the circumstances.

Now it is an undeniable observation that man does not have to commit a crime or hurt another in any way if he doesn't want to. Furthermore, the most severe tortures and even the threat of death cannot compel him to do what he makes up his mind not to do. Since this observation is mathematically undeniable, the words free will, which signify this, are also absolutely true because they symbolize what mathematical perception cannot deny, and here lies the unconscious source of all the dogmatism and confusion because man is not caused or compelled to do anything he makes up his mind not to do.

The words "free will" contain an assumption or fallacy for they imply that if man is not compelled to do anything against his will, it must be preferred of his own free will. This is one of those logical, not mathematical conclusions. Consequently, determinism was faced with an impossible task because it assumed that heredity and environment caused man to choose evil when it was obvious that nothing, absolutely nothing could cause him to do what he makes up his mind not to do. He was not caused or compelled to commit a crime; he did it of his own free will; he wanted to do it, he didn't have to. The words cause and compel are the perception of an improper or fallacious relation because in order for them to be developed and have significance it was absolutely necessary that the words "free will" be born as their opposite. But none of these words actually describe reality unless interpreted properly. The expression, "I did it of my own free will" is perfectly correct when it is understood to mean, "I did it because I wanted to do it; nothing compelled or caused me to do it since I could have acted otherwise had I desired." But the truth of the matter is that at any particular moment of time the motion of man is not free for all life obeys an invariable law, which I shall prove in an undeniable manner. It is extremely important, however, that you understand the expression "I did it of my own free will" is correct, but in no way indicates that man's will is free. In fact, I shall use it frequently myself.

During every moment of a person's existence he is carried along, completely beyond his control, on the wings of time or life. He cannot stop himself from getting older, and is compelled to either live or commit suicide if not satisfied with life; can anyone disagree?

It is taken for granted you understand that a great many motions of man are under the normal compulsion of living and therefore do not play any part in what pertains to the belief in free will because no choice is involved; consequently, these are not my concern. For example, free will does not hold any person responsible for what he does in an unconscious state like hypnosis, nor does it believe that man can be blamed for growing, aging, sleeping, eating, defecating, urinating, etc. Obviously, a great part of our lives offers no choice, and therefore it is unnecessary to prove that these actions, which come under the compulsion of living, are beyond control.

Since it is mathematically impossible for man to be both dead and alive at the same time, and since it is mathematically impossible for a person to commit suicide unless dissatisfied with life, we are given the ability to demonstrate a revealing and undeniable relation.

Life is all motion and never satisfied to remain in one spot forever and always. Every motion of life, from the beating heart to the slightest reflex action, from all inner to outer movements of the body, indicates that life is never *satisfied* or content to remain in one position for always, which is death.

I shall now call the present moment of life or time *here,* for the purpose of mathematical clarification, and the next moment coming up *there.* You are now standing on this present moment of time called *here* and are given two alternatives: either live or kill yourself; either move to the next spot called *there* or remain right where you are without moving a hair's breadth, which is death or *here.* Which do you prefer, *here* or *there,* death or life? If you are still reading, it is obvious and mathematically undeniable that you are not satisfied to stay in one position forever and always which is death, and prefer moving off that spot *here* to *there,* which motion is life. Consequently, the motion of life, which is any motion from *here* to *there,* is a movement, however slight or imperceptible, away from that which dissatisfies; otherwise, had you been satisfied to remain *here* in this one position which is death, you would never have moved to *there.* Since the motion of life constantly moves away from *here* to *there,* which motion is an expression of dissatisfaction with death or a motion away from that which dissatisfies, it must obviously move constantly in the direction of satisfaction. This reasoning is completely mathematical in every way and does not require your approval for its validity. However, it is not imperative that you grasp these relations the first time around, as the rest of the book will confirm their veracity. My suggestion is to take your time and study them anyway, for they cannot be denied unless by someone who does not understand this reasoning at all. Three is to six what four is to eight, but if you cannot understand this relation, your inability does not invalidate the truth.

This simple demonstration proves conclusively that from moment to moment all through his life man can never move in the direction of dissatisfaction, and that his every motion, conscious or unconscious, is a natural effort to get rid of some dissatisfaction or move to greater satisfaction; otherwise, as has been shown, not being dissatisfied, he could never move from *here* to *there*. Every motion of life expresses dissatisfaction with the present position. Scratching is the effort of life to remove the dissatisfaction of the itch, as urinating, defecating, sleeping, working, playing, mating, etc., are unsatisfied needs of life pushing man always in the direction of satisfaction. It is easy in many cases to recognize things that satisfy, such as money when funds are low, but it is extremely difficult at times, especially when the relation of words has never been understood adequately, to understand the innumerable subconscious factors often responsible for the malaise of dissatisfaction. Consequently, although your mind is still unable to grasp these relations, this demonstration also proves conclusively that man's will is not free, but let us put this to a mathematical test.

Supposing you wanted very much of two alternatives, A, which we shall designate something considered evil by society, instead of B, the humdrum of your regular routine; could you possibly pick B at that particular moment of time if A is preferred as a better alternative when nothing could dissuade you from your decision, not even the threat of the laws? Supposing the clergy wanted of two alternatives, A, which shall now represent something considered good, instead of B, that which is judged evil; is it possible for them to prefer the latter when the former is available as an alternative? If it is utterly impossible to choose B when one of the two must be chosen, are they not *compelled* by their very nature to prefer A; and how can they be free when the favorable difference between A and B is the compulsion of their choice and the motion of life in the direction of greater satisfaction? To be free, according to the definition of free will, man would be able to prefer of two alternatives — either the one he wants or the one he doesn't want, which is an absolute impossibility because selecting what one doesn't want when what one does want is available as an alternative is a motion in the direction of dissatisfaction. For example, it would permit a woman to spend on a dress she does not want when a dress she does want is available as an alternative. If she does not want either dress, she is <u>compelled to prefer</u> the one that is the least undesirable of the two; therefore, her choice in this comparison is the most preferable or satisfying under her particular circumstances.

Supposing you were taken prisoner in wartime for espionage and condemned to death, but mercifully given a choice of two exists: A is the painless hemlock of your philosopher Socrates, while B is death by having your head held under water; which do you prefer, and have I given you a choice? Is it humanly possible to prefer exit B if A is offered as an alternative? Yet it is stated that good or evil can be chosen without compulsion or necessity despite the obvious fact that there is a tremendous amount of compulsion. Once it is understood that life is compelled to move in the direction of satisfaction, and two such alternatives are presented, what choice can you possibly have but to accept the lesser of two evils? Since it is absolutely impossible to prefer B as long as A is available as an alternative, although it could be chosen to something still worse, are you not compelled, completely beyond your control in this set of circumstances, to prefer A; and since the definition of free will states that man can choose good or evil without compulsion or necessity, how is it possible for the will of man to be free when choice is under a tremendous amount of compulsion since B was evil and could not be selected in this comparison of alternatives? "But this is ridiculous," you might reply, "for you are not giving us any choice." I most certainly am giving you a choice, and if you are free, you should be able to choose B just as well as A.

The word choice is very misleading for it assumes that man has two or more possibilities but in reality this is a delusion because the direction of life, always moving towards satisfaction, compels man to prefer of differences what he considers better for himself; and when two or more alternatives are presented for his consideration he is compelled, by his very nature, to prefer not that one which is considered by him worse, but what gives every indication of being better for the particular set of circumstances involved. The purpose of thinking things through is to avoid, as much as possible, making a mistake, which is hindsight recognition of what should have been done where the reactions of others are concerned. The purpose of choice is to compare meaningful differences to decide which alternative is preferable. A and B, representing small or great differences, are compared. The comparison is absolutely necessary to know which is preferable. The difference, which is considered favorable, regardless of the reason, is the compulsion of greater satisfaction, which makes one of them an impossible choice in this comparison because it gives less satisfaction. Consequently, since B is an impossible choice, you are not free to choose A, for your preference is a natural compulsion of the direction of life over which you have absolutely no control. The word choice itself indicates there are preferable differences, otherwise there would be no choice in the matter at all as with A and A. Choosing, or the comparison of differences, is an integral part of man's nature, but he is compelled to prefer of alternatives the one he considers better for himself. Consequently, even though he chooses various things all through the course of his life, he is never given any choice at all. Are you beginning to see how words have deceived you?

Supposing to demonstrate that man's will is free, you show that although you prefer a yellow to a red apple, you are going to choose and eat the red; do you honestly think this demonstrates freedom of the will? Isn't it obvious that regardless of the reason you decided to eat the red apple, this choice, at that moment of time, gave you greater satisfaction; otherwise, you would have definitely selected the yellow?

How many times in your life have you remarked, "It makes no difference" or "You give me no choice?" Just because some differences are so obviously superior in value that no hesitation is required to decide which of the alternatives is preferable, while other differences need a more careful consideration, doesn't change the direction of life which moves always and ever towards satisfaction. The truth of the matter is that all through life man is compelled to choose what he considers not evil but good for himself; but who has the right to judge what is good or evil for another when a particular set of circumstances may decide one to prefer what he knows is wrong in the eyes of society yet considered good for himself since the alternative is still worse. What you may judge bad for yourself doesn't make it so for another, especially when it is remembered that a juxtaposition of differences in each case presents alternatives which affect choice.

Man has two possibilities that are reduced to the common denominator of one. Either he doesn't have a choice because no choice is involved, as with aging, and then it is obvious that he is under the compulsion of living, regardless of what his particular motion at any moment might be, or he has a choice and then is given two or more alternatives of which he is compelled, by the motion of his life, to prefer the one he considers better for himself, whether it is the lesser of two evils, the greater of two goods, or a good over an evil. Therefore, it is mathematically impossible for the will of man to be free. It was also mathematically impossible for any previous stage of your development to have understood the deeper factors involved, which were necessary for an adequate solution, just as it was impossible for atomic energy to have been discovered prior to when it was, because the deeper relations were not perceived. Consequently you have been compelled to blame, criticize and punish as the only possible alternative when judged by your undeveloped mind; but at last you will be granted understanding which reveals a pattern of harmony in the mankind system equal in every way with the mathematical accuracy of the solar system, and you are in for the greatest series of beneficent changes in your entire existence, which must come about as a matter of necessity the very moment this entire book is understood. This and the next chapter only scratch the surface while laying the foundation.

Man, as a part of nature or God, has been unconsciously developing at a mathematical rate, and during every moment of his progress he was doing what he had to do because he had no choice. But this does not mean that he was caused to do anything against his will, for the word cause, like choice and past, is very misleading as it implies that something other than man himself is responsible, like environment and heredity, which do not cause; they are man's actions; or like God, who does not cause, he is. Your mother and father did not cause; they are your birth. Nothing in the past can possibly *cause* what occurs in the present, for all we ever have is the present; the past and future are only words that describe a deceptive relation. Four is not caused by two plus two; it is that already. Nothing causes man to build cities, develop scientific achievements, write books, compose music, go to war, argue and fight, commit terrible crimes, pray to God, for these things are mankind already at a particular stage of his development. These activities or motions are the natural entelechy of man who is always developing, correcting his mistakes, and moving in the direction of greater satisfaction. He is constantly compelled by his nature to make choices, decisions, and prefer of whatever is available during each lifetime that which he considers better for himself. If he finds that a discovery like the electric bulb is for his benefit in comparison to candlelight, he is compelled to prefer it, for his motion, just being alive, is always in the direction of greater satisfaction. But this knowledge, this discovery that man's will is not free, was not available to you before this, and what it reveals as each individual becomes conscious of his true nature is something fantastic to behold, for it not only gives ample proof that God is a definite reality, but it will also put an immediate end to all evil around Earth.

To say God is good is a true observation, for nothing in this universe, when the mathematical relations are perceived, is evil, which is only a word to describe the hurt in human relations. The fact that your theologians could never reconcile good and evil with a God that caused everything, compelled them for satisfaction to give birth to Satan or some other force of darkness, in order to continue believing in the goodness of God. How was it possible for your people to believe that Christ and Moses were not one whit better than Hitler, or for the Jews to believe that God exterminated six million of their people? Do you see how easy it is for words to confuse unless clarified with the perception of mathematical relations?

The belief in free will was compelled to come about as a corollary of evil because it was impossible to blame God for man's deliberate crimes. Therefore, it was stated that man did not have to do what he did because he was endowed with a special faculty which allowed him to choose between good and evil. It never dawned on your theologians and philosophers that man's choice of what he considered better for himself, even though it may have been evil when judged by others, came about in direct obedience to his nature or God's will, who had reasons you were not supposed to understand — until now.

Though it is true that man must always prefer that which he considers good, not evil, for himself when the latter is offered as an alternative (but remember the words good and evil are judgments of what others think is right and wrong, not symbols of reality), it was necessarily misinterpreted because of the general ignorance that prevailed. But the amazing thing is that this ignorance, this conflict of ideas, ideologies, and desires, theology's promulgation of free will, the millions that criticized determinism as ridiculous, everything was exactly as it was supposed to be. It was impossible for man on your planet or any other to have acted differently because the mankind system is obeying this invariable law of satisfaction which makes the motions of all life just as harmonious as the solar system; but these systems are not caused by, they are these laws. This universe is a mathematical whole which includes man who has been steadily gravitating in an unconscious manner towards the Golden Age which many of your prophets foresaw; but now no more prophesies are necessary for this long-awaited, wonderful moment you have been looking forward to with great anticipation has arrived at last. There will take place a virtual miracle of transformation as each person consciously realizes what it means that his will is not free, which has not yet been revealed.

The knowledge that man's will is not free and what this means, which will be revealed shortly, is your long-sought elixir of alchemy, for the baser metals of human nature are going to be magically transmuted into the pure gold of genuine happiness for every individual on your planet. It is also that long sought standard and touchstone of truth and reality.

CHAPTER 2 — The Great Impasse of Blame

Just think of this tremendous wisdom! Here is versatile man — writer, composer, artist, inventor, scientist, philosopher, theologian, architect, builder, mathematician, chess player, murderer, prostitute, thief, etc. — whose will is absolutely and positively not free, yet compelled by his very nature to believe that it is, and solely for the benefit of developing mind and matter which could not have been accomplished otherwise; and then permitted, after reaching a sufficient degree of development (the discovery of atomic energy) to perceive the necessary relations that will is not free, which perception is utterly impossible without the development and absolutely necessary for the inception of your Golden Age. Where in all history have you ever seen anything so fantastic?

Now once it is established beyond a shadow of doubt that will is not free because life is constantly moving in the direction of satisfaction completely beyond control (this is an invariable law which cannot be denied or disproven by anyone anywhere), compelling man to always prefer of available alternatives that which he, not someone else, considers better for himself, it becomes mathematically impossible to blame him for anything he does, regardless of what is done. Though this is an undeniable corollary, how is it humanly possible not to hold him responsible for murder, rape, the killing of six million people, etc.? Does this mean that you are supposed to condone these crimes or turn the other cheek? Besides, what will prevent you from blaming and punishing despite the fact that will is not free — if it gives you greater satisfaction? Just because man's will is not free is certainly not a sufficient explanation as to why there should be no blame. At this very point lies the crux of a problem that has kept free will in power since time immemorial. The solution, however, only requires the perception and extension of relations which cannot be denied; and this mathematical corollary, that man is not to blame for anything at all, is a key to the infinite wisdom of God which will unlock a treasure so wonderful that you will be compelled to catch your breath in absolute amazement. But your mind is so utterly confused with words that it will require painstaking clarification to clear away the logical cobwebs of ignorance that accumulated through the years out of necessity.

Now to solve this enigma regarding the corollary, Thou Shall Not Blame (for this seems mathematically impossible), it is extremely important to go through a deconfusion process regarding words by employing a mathematical relation, which can be empirically verified. Consequently, as was earlier pointed out and to reveal this relation, it is an absolutely undeniable observation that man does not have to commit a crime or do anything to another person unless he wants to. Even the most severe tortures and the threat of death cannot make him do what he makes up his mind not to do, where other people are involved. He is not caused or compelled against his will to hurt another by his environment and heredity but prefers this action because at that moment he considers it better for himself for one reason or another. It gives him greater satisfaction by better removing the dissatisfaction of the moment, which is a normal compulsion of his nature over which he has absolutely no control. But though it is a mathematical, undeniable law that nothing can compel man to do to another what he makes up his mind not to do (this is an extremely crucial point), he is nevertheless under a compulsion to do everything he does.

He is not compelled to work at a job he doesn't like or remain in a country against his will; he actually wants to do the very things he dislikes simply because the alternative is considered worse in his opinion or the lesser of two evils. You can lead a horse to water, but you can't make him drink unless he wants to. Was it humanly possible to make Gandhi and his people do what they did not want to do when unafraid of death, which was considered the lesser of two evils? Consequently, when any person says he was compelled to do what he did against his will, that he really didn't want to do it but had to (and innumerable of your words and expressions say this), he is obviously confused by words and unconsciously dishonest with himself because everything man does to another is done, as was mathematically demonstrated, of his own free will, which only means that his preference gave him greater satisfaction at that moment of time for one reason or another; but remember, this desire of one thing over another is a compulsion beyond control for which he cannot be blamed. So bear in mind now, for this is that very crucial point I find necessary to repeat; man is never compelled to do what he doesn't want to do, but is compelled to do everything he does. This reveals that he has mathematical control over the former, but absolutely none over the latter. All I am doing is clarifying your terms so that you are not confused, but make sure you understand this mathematical difference before proceeding further.

Consequently, if man were to say, "I couldn't help myself because my will is not free," which demonstrates vividly how utterly confused your philosophical minds have always been, or should he make any effort to shift his responsibility to heredity, environment, God, or something else for the many things he wants to do, he is obviously lying or being dishonest with himself because absolutely nothing is forcing him, <u>against his will</u>, to do what he doesn't want to do, for over this he has mathematical control. The belief in free will (again take note of your confusion) ironically enough permitted justification, excuses, extenuating circumstances and the shifting of guilt to someone or something else as the cause, to absorb part if not all the responsibility, which allowed man to absolve his conscience in a world of right and wrong and get away with murder in a figurative sense — the very things which the knowledge that will is not free positively prevents as you will see.

It should be obvious that all your judgments of what is right and wrong in human conduct are based upon an ethical standard such as the Ten Commandments, which came into existence out of God's will as did everything else, and consequently you have come to believe, through a fallacious association of symbols, that these words which judge the actions of others are accurate. But in reality when murder is committed it is neither wrong nor right, just what someone at a certain point in his life considered better for himself under circumstances which included the judgment of others and the risks involved; and when the government or personal revenge retaliates by taking this person's life, this too was neither right nor wrong, just what gave greater satisfaction. Neither the government or the murderer are to blame for what each judged better under their particular set of circumstances; but whether they will decide to think and react as before will depend not on any moral values, not on habit, not on custom, not on any standards of right and wrong, but solely on whether the conditions, under which they were previously motivated, remain the same, and they do not remain as before because the knowledge that man's will is not free reveals facts never before understood.

Because of this general confusion with words, through which you have been compelled to see a distorted reality, it appears at first glance that the dethronement of free will would allow man to shift his responsibility all the more and take advantage of not being blamed to excuse or justify any desires heretofore kept under control by the fear of punishment and public opinion which judged his actions in accordance with standards of right and wrong; but this is a superficial perception of inaccurate reasoning simply because it is mathematically impossible to shift your responsibility, to excuse or justify getting away with something, when you know in advance that you will not be blamed for what you do. Now observe this very carefully:

Is it possible for you to say, "I couldn't help myself because man's will is not free," when you know in advance that *no one* will blame or judge your action regardless of what you do? I repeat, think about this very carefully because it is another crucial point. If you try to justify or excuse your action, it is an indication that the person to whom you are presenting this justification must consider the action wrong in some way; otherwise, there would be no need for it. If you do what others judge to be right, is it necessary to lie or offer excuses? It is only possible to shift your responsibility with excuses and justification when you are held responsible by a code of standards that criticizes you for doing something considered wrong by others. They are interested to know why you could do such a thing, which compels you for satisfaction to think up a reasonable excuse to extenuate the circumstances and mitigate their unfavorable opinion of your action. But once it is realized that *no one* henceforth will blame your doing whatever you desire to do, regardless of what is done — because your action will be considered a compulsion over which you have no control — it becomes mathematically impossible to blame something or someone for what *you know you have done* or shift your responsibility in any way.

The fact that man was held responsible for doing what others considered wrong and evil, and the fact that he desired to do this, compelled him, as a motion in the direction of satisfaction, to blame various factors or causes for the many things he desired to do that were considered wrong since he didn't like to assume full responsibility for being in the wrong. But the very moment the dethronement of free will prevents man from blaming man, he is also prevented from excusing or justifying his own actions, which compels him, completely beyond his control but of his own free will, not only to assume full responsibility for everything he does but to be absolutely honest with himself and others. How is it humanly possible for you to desire lying to me or to yourself when your actions are not being judged by others; and how is it possible for you to shift your responsibility when no one holds you responsible? This is an undeniable observation, but though it demonstrates that man's responsibility is mathematically increased, how is it humanly possible not to judge, not to criticize, not to blame and punish those acts of crime when we know that man was not compelled to do them if he didn't want to. If someone kidnapped and killed your child, how is it possible not to hate the individual responsible, not to judge this as an act of evil, not to desire some form of revenge? This has always been the greatest stumbling block that kept free will on the throne until the present time. But this enigma is easily reconciled when it is understood that the mathematical corollary, God's commandment Thou Shall Not Blame, does not apply to anything after it is done, only before. Once you have been hurt it is normal and natural to seek some form of retaliation for this is a source of satisfaction which is the direction life is compelled to take. Therefore, the knowledge that man's will is not free cannot possibly prevent the hate and blame which you have been compelled to live with all these many years as a consequence of these terrible crimes and other forms of hurt, yet God's mathematical law cannot be denied for man is truly not to blame for anything he does notwithstanding, so obviously a still deeper analysis is required.

The solution lies in the fact that the people truly responsible for all the evil, hurt and crime, for which they cannot be held responsible, are actually unconscious of this responsibility, and instead blame an individual who is not at fault for the very things of which they are innocently guilty. Therefore, the problem is to bring to the surface, with a mathematical, infallible line of demarcation, these hidden facts. Your philosopher Socrates grasped this when he said: "I know that I don't know; other men don't know either, but think they know." But we on Mars know that we know, for the actual responsibility lies with everyone who judges and tacitly blames the actions of another before anything is even done. However, this advance blame is not only contained in your customs, conventions, morals and laws, but in the very words that describe fallacious differences of value which permit superior, inferior, better, worse, good, bad, and innumerable other words and expressions to be used in relation to different individuals.

Every time you ask someone to do you a favor, you are tacitly blaming in advance the possibility of being refused. You are judging what is right for someone else, judging that his desire should be to do you this favor. Mathematical proof that any request for a favor is advance blame is the undeniable fact that you would never ask if you knew positively it would be refused. Consequently, by asking, you are blaming *the possibility* of being disappointed. When you give advice or tell others what to do, you are blaming in advance their desire to be different than what you think is better for them. When you ask a question, you are blaming in advance *the possibility* that it may not be answered. When you show a sign of fear, you are tacitly blaming *the possibility* that someone may harm you even before anything is done; when you express an opinion, you are unconsciously blaming a different point of view. All locks, bolts, keys, weapons, jails, and laws are forms of advance blame because they blame *the possibility* of a wrongful action occurring, thus offering the advance justification to do that very thing. Every time you use a word or expression that judges what the desire of another person should be, or judges how he should act, dress, walk, talk, live, etc., are advance forms of blame. But the question arises, even though God reveals in a mathematical manner that man is not to blame for anything he has ever done, and even though he explicitly states Thou Shall Not Blame, how is it humanly possible for this Great Transition to come about when this advance blame itself, this judging of what is right for others, is such a tremendous source of satisfaction and actually supports millions upon millions of people in their effort to earn a living? The only thing that could make government, religion, the unions, and everyone else give up this judging of what is right for others (and I can't enumerate everything here) is when the alternative to this is still worse, but up until the present time, the knowledge to reveal this great power was not available. You have not been aware that this unconscious judging of what is right for others actually encouraged and justified the very things you didn't want, but take note of the most fantastic wisdom.

At this present moment of time or life you are standing on this spot called *here* and are constantly in the process of moving to *there*. You know as a matter of positive knowledge that nothing, no one can cause or compel you to do anything to another you don't want to do, and this other who is standing on this spot called *there* to which you plan to move from *here*, also knows positively that you cannot be blamed for your motion from *here* to *there*, regardless of what is done. Now if you know as a matter of positive knowledge that not only I but everyone on your planet will never blame or punish you for hurting me in some way, because you know that we are compelled to completely excuse what is beyond your control, is it mathematically possible (think about this carefully) for you to derive any satisfaction whatever from the contemplation of this hurt when you know beyond a shadow of doubt that no one, including myself, will ever hold you responsible, ever criticize your action, ever desire to hurt you in return for doing what is completely beyond your control? But remember, you haven't hurt me yet, and you know that you do not have to hurt me unless you want to; consequently, your motion from *here* to *there* is still within your control. Therefore the moment it fully dawns on you that this hurt, should you go ahead with it, will not be blamed, criticized or judged in any way because no one wants to hurt you for doing what must be considered a compulsion beyond your control, you are compelled, completely of your own free will or desire, to relinquish this desire to hurt me because it can never give you any satisfaction under these conditions, which proves that A, everybody on your planet, has the power to control B, everybody else, by letting B know, as is being done with this book, that no one will ever be blamed for anything that is done. The solution is now very obvious because the advance knowledge that man will not be blamed for anything he desires to do, mathematically prevents those very acts for which blame and punishment were previously necessary. Instead of being able to absolve your conscience by justifying an act of crime or some other form of hurt, which permitted the shifting of your responsibility while encouraging the crime (are you confused?), the knowledge that your will is not free and what this means actually prevents you from deriving any satisfaction from the contemplation of this hurt to another by the realization that you will not be blamed, criticized or punished for this act. Let me clarify this another way.

Turning the other cheek, which also proves in a mathematical manner that man's will is not free, absolutely prevents the second cheek from being struck because it is impossible, as the people of India demonstrated, to get satisfaction from continuing to hurt those who refuse to fight back, but many were killed just by being struck on the first cheek. My imparting the knowledge that no one will again blame you in any way, judge your actions, or tell you what to do, mathematically prevents your first cheek from being struck, which is necessary in a world of atomic energy where an entire nation can be wiped out by being struck on the first cheek. However, there is one vital point that appears contradictory and needs clarification.

If the knowledge that man's will is not free is supposed to prevent that for which blame and punishment were previously necessary, and if, as was already stated, a person who saw his child deliberately kidnapped and killed would be compelled to desire revenge as a normal reaction in the direction of satisfaction, how can this knowledge prevent some form of revenge? Just because you have learned that man's will is not free is not a sufficient explanation as to why you should not want to cut out the heart of this criminal with a knife, so once again, we must understand what God means when he mathematically instructs us not to blame.

When the knowledge in this book is released and understood, every person, as always, will be standing on this moment of time or life called *here*, and so to speak, preparing to move to the next spot called *there*. Consequently you will be made aware that the person who kidnapped and killed your child, or did some other form of hurt which occurred prior to the release of this knowledge and regardless of how much you hate and despise what was done, will never blame in any way your desire for revenge, which means that he will never run and hide to avoid your vengeance because this act of fear in itself is a form of tacit blame; and when it fully dawns on you that he will never make any effort to fight back no matter what you do to him, never lift a hand to stop whatever you desire to do, it becomes impossible for you to derive any satisfaction from revenge under these new conditions, especially when you know that he will never again be permitted, by his realization that he will never be blamed, to do to another what was originally done to yourself. This allows your Great Transition to get underway, as you will see in greater detail very shortly, without any fear of harm.

The potential kidnapper or criminal, who is standing on this moment of time called *here* when this knowledge is released and before the act is done, is prevented from further contemplation of his crime by the realization that he will never be blamed, judged, criticized, or punished for this act, and by the removal of all forms of tacit blame which unconsciously gave him the motivation and justification, thereby compelling him to get greater satisfaction in his motion to *there,* by giving up what he was contemplating.

Up until the present time on your planet there was nothing powerful enough to prevent man from risking his life to satisfy a desire, regardless of who got hurt, because the satisfaction of possible success outweighed the dissatisfaction of possible failure; but when he becomes conscious that a particular reaction of not being blamed by the entire world will be the response to his action regardless of what it is, he will be compelled, completely beyond his control but of his own free will, to refrain from what he now foresees can give him absolutely no satisfaction.

Time and again, a person seeking personal revenge has experienced this control of his desire, but never in the degree to which our slide rule permits your Great Transition to get underway. When it fully dawns on him in an absolutely undeniable manner that the person he wishes to hurt in return will never desire to retaliate with further hurt what was done to him, he is compelled to lose his desire for revenge because it is impossible to derive any satisfaction from the advance knowledge that he will be excused by everyone for his act of retaliation. The full realization that he can no more justify this act of revenge because no one will consider it wrong, that he can do what he wishes to this person without any form of justification, that everyone is compelled of their own free will (by the release of this knowledge) to completely excuse what is definitely not his responsibility — although he knows it would be — makes him desire to forgo what he knows he does not have to do if he doesn't want to. He knows he is not under any compulsion to do what has not yet been done, and when he becomes aware that no one henceforth will judge his actions, that he is completely free from the trammels of public opinion to do, without the slightest fear of criticism, whatever he thinks is better for himself, that he will not even be punished by the laws, it becomes mathematically impossible for him to desire hurting this other person under these conditions, regardless of what was done to him. It would be equivalent to deriving satisfaction from continuing to beat up an individual who, though fully able to fight back, refuses to lift a hand in his own defense.

In your world of free will, man blamed man and excused himself. In your new world about to unfold, man will be excused by man for everything he does and will be compelled of his own free will to hold himself responsible without justification. Once man knows that he is truly responsible for what others will be compelled to excuse and he would be unable to justify, he is given no choice but to forgo the contemplation of what he foresees can give him no satisfaction. But remember, it is not the knowledge that man's will is not free that compels you to give up this judging in advance what is right for others, otherwise your government, your unions, your religions, all your writers who make a living expressing their opinions as to what is right and wrong with the world, with love, marriage, children, business, education, etc., would suddenly give up their manner of earning a living which is a mathematical impossibility. Do you think that the manufacturers of candles and other inferior forms of lighting wanted to give up what gave them a source of income when electricity was discovered? They were compelled to adjust because they couldn't find a market for their obsolete products except on a smaller scale. Do you think the adulterers want to give up their fun, the single males the pleasure of sexual intercourse before marriage? Do you think the people who are getting wealthy on the sweat, brawn, tears, and insecurity of extremely low wages will give up this just because God thunders down from heaven — Thou Shall Not Blame? Do you think that religion will willingly give up its great power and influence because man's will is not free, which reveals that God is a mathematical reality? The truth of the matter is that everyone will be compelled of his own free will to give up anything that hurts another in any way simply because this hurt will be considered worse under the new conditions. This, my friends, is the great secret of God's infinite wisdom, which gives man no choice and allows the inception of your Golden Age to get underway very smoothly. But the problem is very deep-rooted and involved, which makes it necessary to treat every aspect of your lives in a separate manner. This and the first chapter only laid the groundwork.

Now the problems that confront you at this particular moment are identical to what we experienced on Mars many years ago, but God's mathematical slide rule and standard, his magic elixir Thou Shall Not Blame (Thou Shall Not Judge what is right for another), when understood to apply only before something is done, will adequately solve every one. You can prepare yourselves to say goodbye to all the hurt and evil that came into existence out of necessity.

I shall begin with the world of love and marriage, then go on to children and parents. Thence we shall attack (my slide rule and I) the almost insurmountable problems of government, business, education, and last but not least, though our magic elixir will not apply here, I shall reveal something about death in a mathematical, undeniable manner which will make every reader very happy. Don't you think it strange that of all the millions of years Earth has been in existence (and what is a million years when the words through which you see this relation are clarified) you, of all people, should have been born to see the universe now; why weren't you born 5000 years ago, or why shouldn't you be born in the future? My friends, you are in for quite a pleasant surprise, but your mind is so filled with words like spirit, soul, reincarnation, heaven, etc., which have absolutely no meaning whatever, that you are terribly confused, especially those who think they know. You will soon learn that there is absolutely nothing to fear in death, which in itself will revolutionize your lives, but everything is related, so please bear with me since I cannot put everything down at one time. As I said, you will catch your breath in utter amazement at the infinite wisdom that governs this universe, and you will be given no choice but to change your ways.

PART TWO

The extension of a mathematical relation into the world of boys and girls, husbands and wives, parents and children

CHAPTER 3 — The World of Love

CHAPTER 4 — Marriage

CHAPTER 5 — Children

CHAPTER 3 — The World of Love

It must be constantly borne in mind that no problem exists in your relationship with each other unless someone is being hurt in a concrete, not imaginary, manner. There is nothing morally wrong (these are only words) in committing adultery or getting a divorce, having sexual intercourse before marriage, etc., but when innumerable people have their heart broken and cut out with the knife of unrequited love then it is apparent that those who lose in this game, even though it may be better to have loved and lost than never to have loved at all, are very unhappy individuals because they have lost the very person they wanted to win. Consequently, every single boy and girl is compelled to desire learning the mathematical secret of how to prevent this great hurt to themselves because their own happiness is at stake. If man's will was free, these potential losers could exercise no control over the others who would be free to hurt them; but they are not free and will be mathematically controlled so that no desire to hurt or break another's heart will ever arise again.

At the very heart of your problem is this fallacious difference that exists in the extremes of beauty and ugliness (these are words with no meaning), which permits the development of a one-sided romance. Included in these fallacious differences are words like dumb, stupid, smart, brilliant, educated, genius, which allow those who feel that these apply to them to consider themselves either inferior or superior. Consequently, when a handsome man considers himself extremely educated and brilliant because others consider him so, he is bound to have more than his share of female admirers, and since it is impossible for him to marry everyone, there are bound to be those who lose and get hurt. Everyone likes to be admired, but the moment these more attractive males and females are desired even before any sexual relation takes place, they discover a lack of desire on their own part to possess what they can have for the asking (that is marriage), which convinces them that they are not in love. This is a very serious problem because these fallacious differences actually prevent the blossoming of mutual love, and they also give rise to innumerable arguments after marriage since this feeling of superiority, in one form or another, always imposes a resentful feeling of inferiority. Consequently, the very moment a girl or boy sees that they are admired by the opposite sex a little bit more than it is returned, this other is placed at a disadvantage by being unconsciously considered inferior, and the more this feeling of love is shown, the more they will be uncertain that they are in love. Unconsciously they feel that this other person would be getting the better of the deal, and so, since it is difficult to desire the possession of what is already possessed if they want to get married, they keep this other on a string, so to speak, while they search for someone with whom they can fall in love, that is someone who will desire them less or consider them inferior. As a result of all this there are many marriages on the rebound, which is a courtship that occurs shortly after a breakup. Very few marriages of a first love ever take place as a consequence of these fallacious differences, and love has become a game to try and make the other fall in love.

Children are taught that they should not rush into marriage because they might end up with someone who is really no good, has no character, no intelligence, nothing to make them really proud. Had they compared by going out with different individuals, they might have gotten someone much finer; but these are only words with no significance on our planet.

Now the ultimate problem of love before marriage revolves around one point — how to prevent all the hurt of unrequited romance, and the solution is how to compel all boys and girls to fall mutually in love with the very first person dated. This appears to be quite a problem, doesn't it? How this is accomplished, how these boys and girls are compelled to have this mutual desire for marriage with their first date, is marvelous to behold and mathematically undeniable. It is important, however, before this is demonstrated to clarify two terms.

In actual reality the word "love" symbolizes a desire for a sexual relation, and this is proven by the fact that it is not possible for a boy or girl to fall in love with someone considered extremely good-looking if they know in advance that this individual was born without any sexual organs which knowledge makes them aware that this person is incapable of giving or receiving sexual satisfaction.

Consequently, the degree of love in courtship varies depending on the extent of possible physical satisfaction. If a boy and girl fall in love at first sight it is obvious they desire to get married so they can indulge their sexual appetite for each other; and if they are in love with someone who does not return this feeling, the intensity of their desire to possess the other will depend on how close they will be allowed to come to this physical possession. The more they are encouraged, the greater will be the feeling of love or the desire to possess. This explains why a person can never fall in love with a movie star at a distance when there is no possibility of sexual satisfaction from this source. It also explains why it would be easy for an idol of stage and screen to be a heartbreaker, for it appears that this individual has so much more to offer. But the meaning of love after marriage or sexual intercourse takes place is a horse of another color, for the intensity of their love for each other depends solely on the degree of passionate satisfaction, which proves conclusively that the greater the sexual satisfaction, the stronger will be their love; and this demonstrates why there are so many divorces and so much adultery. Most couples on your planet remain together not because they are still in love, but only because it is the lesser of two evils.

Now the other term is "marriage," which, in actual reality, is nothing more than a mutual desire to indulge in sexual intercourse with the ultimate purpose of bearing a child. It is not the granting of a right to indulge in a sexual relation; it is not the obligation that each has to the other; and it has nothing whatever to do with a religious ceremony or exchange of rings; it is only this mutual desire to beget a child, as you will soon have verified.

On your planet, it is possible to get married and divorced without having a sexual relationship, and possible to have the latter without the former. But on Mars, or once the knowledge in this book is understood, it is impossible to get married without having a sexual relation, and impossible to have the latter without the former. How long do you think your single males would remain unmarried if they couldn't have a sexual relationship any other way? Would they offer excuses about college and being out of work? Either our males get married, or they never indulge. Now tell me, have they been given a choice? But how is it possible to bring about such an amazing change? This is accomplished solely with the aid of the knowledge that man's will is not free. However, because your mind is still not attuned to the perception of mathematical relations, I should like to put the horse before the cart by asking you several questions.

What is more important — that a boy and girl get a license to indulge their sexual appetite, have a religious ceremony, the blessing of a theologian, etc., or that they fall mutually in love and live happily ever after? What is more important to the parents — the health and happiness of their children or the moral code? If you were given a choice of marrying the person you love with the certain knowledge that you are sure to find unhappiness, perhaps be made a cuckold and end up getting a divorce, or given an opportunity not to marry the individual as you know the word marriage but instead of unhappiness the greatest happiness imaginable would be your lot all through life, are you given a choice? Wouldn't it be an insult to man's intelligence to criticize and blame a marriage celebrating half a century of genuine happiness, a marriage in which there was never a thought of another sexual partner, a marriage where there was never an argument, just because this young boy and girl decided to get married without a license, without the ceremony and blessing of a rabbi or priest, without the exchange of rings, etc.? Well, are you beginning to look into the mirror of this book and see yourselves for the first time as you really are, for which you cannot be blamed? Criticizing such happiness because this couple didn't conform to your moral code is equivalent to criticizing someone who plays a perfect hand of bridge because he failed to have the cards cut by the person on his right, or equivalent to someone criticizing this book which reveals only the perception of mathematical, undeniable relations, because he feels that a comma is in the wrong place.

It is understandable why a jeweler would not like a change that affects his business because not buying rings associated with engagements and marriage would certainly decrease his profit; and it is understandable why a priest and rabbi would not like any change because they play one of the leading spiritual roles in the nuptial drama, aside from receiving, perhaps, a gratuity of some sort which is also a pleasant ritual. It is understandable why those who are accustomed to criticizing, blaming, and judging others for not conforming to the moral code would not like a change because this would deprive them of the enormous satisfaction they get from condemning what, in their eyes, is wrong. Consequently, it is of the utmost importance to place the horse before the cart so that these unconsciously ignorant people who have been blindly leading you in accordance with God's will can at last see for themselves what they have been doing. Obviously, since no one likes to give up what is a source of satisfaction unless there is a still greater satisfaction to replace this, or unless, in a new juxtaposition of alternatives, it becomes the worse choice, we can only look to the boy and girl themselves for the great change about to take place. They are the only ones involved in this game of love. However, there are rules to this game which have never been understood, but these you are compelled to obey because each person recognizes instantly their mathematical veracity. The sexes will be given no choice as to how they should act towards each other because they will know, beyond a shadow of doubt, what is the better alternative. You have no conception yet of your unconscious ignorance, and if it were not for the fact that no one is to blame for this, the faces of your professors, your intelligentsia, your writers, your geniuses, your experts would turn every color of the rainbow from embarrassment. Can you think of anything more humorous than religion teaching dogmatically that man's will is free? However, to fully understand and appreciate this fantastic metamorphosis — remember, all premarital relations, all adultery, and all divorce are coming to an end out of mathematical necessity — the only thing required of you is to bear constantly in mind what has been revealed in the first two chapters, that man's will is not free and what this means.

Now when a boy and girl reach the age of sex or nubility, with the knowledge that man's will is not free, they will know that it is mathematically impossible for any person to desire hurting them when it is known *in advance* that they will never blame or criticize this hurt, regardless of what is done. Consequently, when a girl falls in love, whether it is returned or not, she is completely unafraid to offer her body because she knows, just as certain as two plus two equals four, that it is absolutely impossible for him to desire to have a sexual relation with her unless he loves her too. She knows that he knows if he made her pregnant, ruined her life, broke her heart, left and never returned, she and no one would ever blame him for doing what he was compelled to do. But he also knows that he is not compelled to break her heart, ruin her life, make her pregnant, leave and never return, unless he wants to, and the realization that she will never hold him responsible for this terrible hurt which he knows would be his responsibility and which he also knows he can prevent if he wants to, makes it mathematically impossible for him to derive any satisfaction from deflowering her under these conditions.

In your new world, he will need to think long and hard before indulging his appetite by constantly considering the possibility of pregnancy and whether he is prepared to take on this financial responsibility should a pregnancy occur. However, since contraception has been helpful in this regard until a couple is ready to bear a child (although we all know accidents can and do occur), it must be remembered that having children (in most cases) comes as a package deal when searching for a suitable mate. If one does not want a child and the other one does, this would need to be expressed beforehand, in which case there would be no consummation. This would prevent any hurt that could arise if this was not made known in advance, since the commitment to marriage for most couples revolves around the desire to have a family. In your present world, if the man only wanted the woman for sex, avoiding pregnancy at all costs would eventually reveal his true feelings: that he never cared for her enough to be the father of her child regardless of words and promises, and when a girl got slapped squarely in the face with the truth, she could not possibly have desired a relationship under these conditions unless she was starving for sex, which would make her an older girl who is doubtful if any males are available to fall in love with her type. But this latter possibility is removed under the changed conditions — along with many of the expressions and words that standardize and judge the value of looks — by the manner in which children will be raised in the new world.

Therefore, when a boy discovers through these mathematical relations that a girl is perfectly willing to go all the way once he has won her love, he recognizes that there is no advantage, in fact, a complete waste of time, to make a girl fall in love with him unless he sees the possibility of loving her; otherwise, he will be forced, of his own free will, to turn down her generosity since it is not a source of satisfaction to hurt this person by ruining her life when he knows *in advance* that she and no one alive will ever blame him for doing what he knows they must excuse and he cannot justify. Consequently, the very moment a boy and girl indulge, they sincerely pledge their love and are married for life, until death do they part, because it is mathematically impossible for either to ever desire leaving when they know this would be a terrible source of hurt for which there would never be any blame or criticism. But, of course, there are other factors involved which will soon be clarified, so please be patient. Now the knowledge of how the girl will react the moment she is in love (and remember the definition) completely revolutionizes dating.

Since the meaning of love before copulation takes place is the possibility of sexual satisfaction, how is it mathematically possible for a boy to desire taking out a girl who does not appeal to him in terms of marriage when he knows, well in advance, that he will be compelled to refuse her body when it is offered? Consequently, he is given no choice but to search for a girl who appears to offer this possibility of sexual satisfaction, which means that when he asks for a date, he is actually proposing, and when she accepts, they are literally engaged to be married.

She knows, when accepting a date (the girl could very well ask the boy — if she wants), that his love for her will increase only by arousing his passion and satisfying his sexual desire, and he knows that her love for him will increase for the same reason. Consequently, they are given no choice, and when his hand begins to wander, instead of checking this motion as a girl was compelled to do on her dates in order to feel clean and decent, she only encourages it all the more while letting her own hand wander. Obviously, they will become extremely passionate and desire to make love, but the girl will desire this very much without the slightest fear that the boy will ever hurt or leave her. Within a few days, they will be madly in love with each other because love is a crescendo of physical satisfaction, from kissing and petting to the ethereal heights of extreme sexual passion. The hotter a girl can make a boy, the more will he be in love, and the hotter a boy can make a girl, the more will she be in love. Is it any wonder so many men and women have turned to adultery and divorce because they found no more sexual passion in their marriage; and is it any wonder why so many girls drove away the boys they liked because they were afraid of what might happen? But this is the way it was supposed to be in the world of free will, though not anymore, unless the boys and girls prefer losing the person they would like to have for a wife or husband.

Under these conditions there is no possibility for unrequited love to develop, no chance for a girl to be swept off her feet and lose her virginity out of wedlock, no chance for a boy and girl to hurt each other in any way. Their mating, which takes place the moment it is mutually desired, is the holiest of all unions because it is steeped in a feeling of mutual respect and love, and no one need ever fear for this couple.

In your present world the advantage always went to the one who made the other fall in love, for then it was possible to take or leave this other. But now the boys and girls recognize that there is no advantage to making someone fall in love unless it can be returned, which makes the sexes do everything in their power to reveal their true feelings, as the desire to have sexual relations depends on loving, not just being loved.

What makes this whole thing so serious is the very fact that the boy knows the girl will never hold him responsible in any way, that he is free to have a good time, leave and never come back no matter how much he hurts her, which makes it mathematically impossible for him to desire even getting close to such a situation unless he really wants to get married. Consequently, he can find no pleasure in kissing someone who does not appeal to him enough for marriage, since this would only create an awkward situation if she were in love with him. Knowing that dating will lead to kissing, kissing to petting and petting will lead to what he cannot do unless in love or ready for marriage, he has no choice but to take out only the girl who offers this possibility of sexual satisfaction. Furthermore, knowing that the girl's parents will never blame him for making her pregnant and will assume the responsibility and expense of raising his child, he is compelled to prepare himself for marriage well in advance so that his decision to make love will not hurt anybody, for he cannot derive even a little bit of satisfaction from being excused for doing what he knows is his responsibility.

There is no such thing in the new world as the right time to start kissing or petting, the right time for marriage, only what is considered right by each couple. These boys and girls will be completely free to do what they consider better for themselves, but the knowledge that man's will is not free doesn't give them any choice and prevents either from ever hurting the other. Consequently, no games will be played, and when a boy asks a girl for a date, he is literally proposing, which means they will begin kissing and petting after a very brief acquaintance. Every couple under these conditions will fall mutually in love with their first date, which makes a marriage ceremony a farce since it serves no purpose other than to make them realize their obligations to each other;

but there will be no obligations henceforth as this blames the desire of another while it encourages and justifies what neither prefers by imposing force.

Under these conditions all the factors truly responsible for premarital promiscuity, adultery, and divorce are removed simply because man is prevented from desiring the very things for which blame and punishment, moral judgment, and criticism were previously necessary. The average boy and girl will be married between 16 and 18 years of age, and there will be no bachelors or spinsters, no broken homes and hearts — even widows and widowers will be a thing of the past as all the causes of premature death are also removed. A boy will have no choice in the matter of marriage, as it will be his only source of sexual satisfaction, which I shall sum up by using mathematical phraseology.

Since the single males who are not in love with the single girls who love them are prevented from indulging without contraception because they consider this decision better for themselves, and are prevented from participating with contraception because the girls who love them consider this choice better for the girls; and since a single female who is not in love with the boy who loves her is prevented from sexual intercourse without contraception because she does not want this boy to be her husband and the father of her child, and is prevented from indulging with contraception because it is impossible for a girl who has never indulged before in any shape or form to desire going out on a date and making love with someone she does not like, love, or desire, it is therefore obvious that the only way these single people can get together sexually — once they understand what it means that man's will is not free — is to fall mutually in love. Consequently the only other sexual outlet for them, other than masturbation, is to indulge with married men and women or the looser, more experienced courtesans and bachelors, but all will be prevented in due time, not only because these will die off while the new marriages get under way but also because of a tremendous change that is about to take place in your very lives as a result of your reading and understanding the rest of the book. It should be obvious that once these young couples lose the desire for another sexual partner, within a relatively short period of time only these marriages will exist, and when a boy can get no sexual outlet except through marriage, he will fall in love, and so will she, with the first person that offers any physical attraction, which, however, will take on new significance as the standards of value, now fallaciously congealed in opinions and words that affect choice, lose their influence while being replaced with personal feelings that are not affected by the judgment of others. Therefore the basis of a sound marriage in the new world will be this physical attraction and satisfaction both experience in the presence of each other, nothing else... not money, education (which is another farce that came into existence out of necessity and will surprise everybody, especially those who consider themselves educated); not social position, religion, color, race, or anything else you care to throw in; only physical attraction and from this foundation the greatest happiness imaginable will be in store for your posterity — which is only yourselves. That's right!... only yourselves, which will be explained, as already mentioned, in the last chapter.

Free will engendered the suave, good-mannered, expertly controlled habits of the conquering, good-looking male, who ensnared with his captivating style many an unsuspecting female. It allowed one girl to keep on a string for an indefinite time many boys who sought her hand in marriage, and who ended up, in many cases, not marrying any of them because she found it difficult desiring to possess what was already hers if she wanted any of them. The word love in your present world not only symbolizes this desire for possession and the stronger emotions of unrequited love, but it is used to justify what could not be done without this justification. A girl who finds terrific pleasure in sexual intercourse with a married man is compelled to justify this act by saying, "I'm in love." About to get married, which, in most cases in your present world, means getting ready for a miserable existence since even those marriages that survive exist unhappily as the lesser of two evils, a man will justify padlocking or wedlocking himself to one person apparently for life by saying, "I'm in love." But this is a completely fallacious perception simply because the girl in bed with the married man is in love with the thrill of sexual satisfaction that has become associated with a particular person, while our bridegroom is very much in love with the prospects that lie ahead — unless he was given a sneak preview. Ask a man who has been married a number of years, "Are you in love with your wife?" and he will reply, "I must be, I'm married ain't I?"

This tremendous need for sex had to be justified in a world of morality, judgment and sin, and the word love served a useful purpose before marriage, and was used to compensate, in an unconscious manner, after marriage. When a husband or wife tells the other they are in love, it only reveals that they are not in love. However, many times the word love was an insufficient justification because innumerable girls found themselves doing what was judged sinful while not being in love, and the consequence was the confessional or psychiatry, both needed to help excrete the accumulation of guilt.

Very few people who get married on your planet actually continue to experience the thrills of love because the height of sexual passion is never experienced afterwards, but the next chapter will reveal that love will increase to a tremendous degree after marriage, never before. You earthlings are so confused that you even think jealousy is a sign of love and have gone out of your way to arouse this emotion, which was used to justify and dissemble a secret, unconscious desire, thinking this would strengthen your marriage or courtship. It arises, however, from a feeling of ownership that tacitly blames and judges what is right for someone else while giving unconscious justification to do that of which one has already been accused. Jealousy originates in going steady, and then grows in intensity from getting engaged to marriage. The first two are a down payment on this right to absolutely possess another individual, and the latter is complete ownership. "I want you" is the meaning of love before this possession takes place, "I almost have you" is the next phase, and "I've got you at last" is the death of love. Why do you think so many jokes are made about marriage if not because it is a sadly humorous situation as you know it? However, it will be changed in a manner marvelous to behold. While jealousy is removed from the world, not because it is a form of blame, but because no one on your planet will ever again have the desire to make another jealous, for this is a motion, under the new conditions, that will render less satisfaction. Seeing what is truly better for himself, not with opinions but mathematical laws, man is given no alternative, unless he prefers what he doesn't want, which is an absolute impossibility.

It is quite humorous to observe that man has been compelled to use reverse psychology since time immemorial as a direct result of believing, consciously or unconsciously, that man's will is free — but he had no choice until now. But now, however, he can choose freely without any interference from your experts, and as a consequence is permitted to get rid of all the evil and hurt nobody wants, only, of course, without having a free choice. Are you beginning to understand how your words have confused your mind?

In this next chapter you will be given an opportunity to observe a newly married couple under the changed conditions as they face life together, knowing for the first time that man's will is not free and what this means, which reveals conclusively why the mathematical corollary, Thou Shall Not Blame, when understood properly, is undeniably better for mankind, giving him no choice.

CHAPTER 4—Marriage

Although it was just demonstrated in a mathematical manner how it is impossible for premarital relations and pregnancies to exist once it is understood that man's will is not free, there are other related problems dealing with words that have not yet been answered only because it is impossible to put everything down at the same time. The solution, however, refers me back to my first chapter to make certain that you understand why the eyes are not a sense organ so I can reveal more clearly the fallacy of words.

It should be obvious to your common sense that the sun exists out in space, like the moon, the stars, your car, television, etc. These objects are real, are completely independent of your perception, and do not exist in your head as some epistemologists have imagined. You see them not because they impinge upon the optic nerve but because they are there to be seen if you care to look. The word does not create the dog as it does heaven, spirit, soul, etc., yet it contains the consciousness of a difference that exists in the external or internal world. The word dog makes you conscious that something existing is not a cat or a cow, but the word heaven plus your fallacious belief that anything is possible makes you conscious of something that might exist.

Remember, there is absolutely nothing that travels from the dog to the optic nerve, although the bark does strike the ears, and this sound is a slide in itself, which then permits the brain to look at this bit of living substance through the many relations that become associated with the sound. As stimuli enter through the four senses and get combined in various relations, they are then projected upon the screen of substance through the eyes which sees everything in relation to what is on the slide. If a child gets frightened by the barking of a dog, this fear is recorded on the slide and photographed in relation, and when a dog is seen, the fear is projected.

Now among human relations there are a tremendous number of differences simply because you yourself are different; consequently, what you experience in your world depends on the slides through which you see your experiences. The words that you learned while growing up and reading many books are your slides which you experienced in context, in relation to certain things, which means that you will use and look through them as these experiences project the relation. Consequently these words or slides represent your consciousness of something you know exists because you see these things with your eyes, and here is the true source of all the confusion, because though the experiences are real and cannot be denied, your understanding of them is fallacious since your brain never photographed a mathematical relation which allowed you to see a discolored version of reality. The very fact that a man like your philosopher Will Durant believes he sees that man's will is free with direct perception, and the very fact that you actually believed you had five senses, amply illustrates what I mean. However, a still deeper analysis is required, which you will now be able to understand.

In the course of many years, you developed words to describe opposites; this was absolutely necessary for your development, but though it is true that death is the opposite of life and determinism is the opposite of free will, tall is not the opposite of short, nor is educated the opposite of uneducated. Brilliance is not the opposite of stupidity, yet these fallacious differences, which you will understand much better when education is discussed, were perceived because you were looking through the slides of these words which were projected realistically onto substance in relation to certain undeniable experiences. Consequently, you actually came to believe that this range of difference between one extreme and the other, between ugliness and beauty, etc., was a part of the real world, and your entire vocabulary was employed to describe this gamut of imaginary differences.

Now, certain opposites represent a range of imaginary values from one extreme to the other. An ugly person, therefore, is automatically at a disadvantage in your society because the opposite sex considers a beautiful or handsome person more attractive. Consequently, this ugly individual is being struck a hurtful blow by the word itself, while the beautiful person can look forward to a much happier existence. A college graduate is considered of greater value and therefore is paid a higher income; besides, he receives greater respect and gets a title like professor or Ph.D., which again places him in a category apart from others. Though it is true he may have read more books, may have learned more words, may have passed to a higher grade than other of his colleagues; yet a laborer may have shoveled more dirt, may have developed greater muscles, may have learned more curse words... for what reason is the one considered more educated? The fallacy lies in the fact that the word education, like beauty, has become associated only with certain differences and represents a judgment of one person in relation to another, but regardless of who is the judge, the word compels him to see through this slide a very intelligent, educated person, while someone else, with a different background, may see an uneducated individual. Most of you know this, but you are unaware that it is absolutely impossible for either individual to see this person for what he really is because the words or slides discolor what actually exists, and only when these very symbols are removed will you begin to get a glimpse of the real world. The unhappiness resulting from these words is both manifold and manifest in the very fact that people develop a complex of inferiority from which stem a host of evils, but much good developed also by permitting or driving those with a feeling of inferiority to develop at an enormous rate in an effort to get rid of what gave them no satisfaction. It is for this very reason that many of your most developed minds were handicapped people, or individuals who never went to school but who recognized their talents by a comparison which spurred them on. But now it is time to draw a mathematical line of demarcation, the line which will reveal how much of what a doctor prescribes is for the benefit of his patient or for his own benefit; how much value exists in a college education for the benefit of the students or for the benefit of the teachers; how much value exists in government for the benefit of the people or for the benefit of the government; how much value exists in religion for the benefit of the congregation or for the benefit of the clergy; how much value exists in socialism, communism, the unions, etc., for the benefit of the people or for the benefit of those in power; how much value there is in being born one type of individual now called beautiful and intelligent, and the other type now called ugly or stupid.

There is much unhappiness in the relation between boys and girls because of these slides through which they are compelled, completely beyond control, to look at each other; and it is obvious that if you have an opportunity to win a beautiful, in preference to an ugly individual, you are given no choice, while the other person is compelled to live in an unhappy world because of your selection. There is also a tremendous amount of unhappiness in marriage due to the very fact that a husband and wife are compelled to see each other through slides that reveal the superiority of one and the inferiority of the other. This is important to understand because it reveals the ultimate source of why many were compelled to be bachelors and spinsters, prostitutes and criminals, why the desire to hurt others arose as the lesser of two evils.

This great transition, however, could never take place without knowing that man's will is not free and what this means, for it is mathematically impossible for a professor to desire giving up his rank of education; and it is impossible for a person to give up the notion that he is more handsome, as these are a definite source of satisfaction which gives them no choice; just as it is mathematically impossible to convince religion that her services will no longer be required along with government. These changes come about out of necessity by revealing in an infallible manner where the responsibility lies for this terrible hurt to others, which is then not blamed, but the great humor lies in the fact that what is accomplished is the very perfection these various organizations have been purporting to bring about.

The man seeking revenge (second chapter) finds great satisfaction in contemplating what he is going to do to get even, but is prevented not because he decides not to blame when learning that man's will is not free, but only because the other person on whom he desires to vent his venom has been given the knowledge of how to prevent this retaliation, while the one seeking revenge knows how to prevent the recurrence of a similar situation.

The great change in words takes place not only as a consequence of the perfect harmony in which children will be raised, but also because you will be made conscious that whenever you use a word that places another in a category of plus, you seriously hurt some individual by putting him in a category of minus, for which you know he and no one will ever blame you. If I call a girl beautiful in the presence of another who is not considered as nice, or whose opinion differs from mine, I am seriously hurting this other person who prevents my desire to hurt her this way by letting me know *well in advance,* through this knowledge, that she will never blame me for this hurt.

Children are scarred so deeply by the ignorance of their parents and teachers who use words like cute, adorable, pretty, precious, lovable, smart, brilliant, a brain, etc., which words do not apply to those who do not receive these compliments, that it is no wonder psychiatry came into existence. This proves conclusively that the expression in the second sentence of the first chapter is completely fallacious, and further reveals how unconscious you have been of your ignorance. Likewise, is the famous expression of Shakespeare proven completely fallacious not only because it is impossible for man to be true to himself when looking through fallacious symbols, but also because it is impossible not to be false to another when you recognize in this dishonesty an advantage to yourself, for your motion is in the direction of greater satisfaction. Only when you see there is no advantage or a still greater benefit by being truthful to others do you desire to mend your ways, but such a preference required knowledge not even available.

As a direct consequence of these fallacious words or slides, it was impossible for a marriage in the world of free will to get off on a completely mutual basis. Even a young couple getting married under the most perfect conditions would end up having arguments, which are not healthy despite your psychologists, because it is impossible, without the knowledge that will is not free, which allows the perception of reality, for two people with their own desires to have a balanced equation. For what reason would Durant consider certain type women as decerebrated dolls, perhaps like the wife of Socrates, if he didn't perceive this difference in intelligence between these females? Now, how is it possible for a genius to live in harmony with his spouse when he considers her intelligence, her education, her wisdom, her common sense, much inferior to his own? What happens when the thrill of her body diminishes; won't he wonder what on earth could have made him take such a woman? This kind of logic compelled philosophers like Nietzsche and Durant to believe that a couple should not be allowed to make too quick a decision about marriage, which only reveals the extent of their unconscious ignorance, for which neither can be blamed.

With this in mind, I shall now attack the problems of marriage and demonstrate, in a completely undeniable manner, God's infinite wisdom as the most perfect relations imaginable between a very young couple become a mathematical reality. Then I shall attack the present problems that exist in marriage, and you will behold a virtual miracle.

It is extremely important to understand at this juncture that when a boy and girl fall mutually in love for the very first time, and consummate their feelings with a complete sexual relation, they are going to desire each other all the more because this exciting thrill of physical contact is a new experience that becomes associated with one particular person to whom they look for satisfaction. Consequently, both will look forward with great anticipation to their next meeting and will desire the passion and thrill of this relationship as often as possible. Soon, each will be dependent on the other for what the body now craves, and if this were stopped as happened frequently in the world of free will for various reasons — which occasioned the serious consequences of unrequited love — it would be the worst form of cruelty. Yet there are two individual desires involved, and it is impossible, in the new world, for one person to desire obligating the other, as this is a form of tacit blame, a judgment of what is right for someone else, which cannot be preferred when it is realized that this will only make matters worse. So immediately after marriage (their first sexual relation, which just took place in the previous chapter), they know that they are not under any obligation to the other, that they are free to do whatever is thought better for themselves, which decision must be made of their own free will. Neither, however, at this precise moment in their lives, desires to leave or lose the other, and consequently, they are compelled to prefer learning the mathematical secret of how to arouse the desire of the other to always want them. Even in your present world, you dream in your love stories of getting married and living happily ever after.

Now this radiant wife, who has been falling more and more in love with her husband as they continue making passionate love to each other, as they continue looking forward to the warmth and ecstasy of this sexual satisfaction, knows positively that it is absolutely impossible for her husband to ever desire leaving her, despite the fact that she knows he is not under any obligation to remain and is completely free to do anything he wants to do, just as long as he knows she is definitely in love with him (take your time with this), because she knows that he knows if he left her under these conditions this would break her heart for which he would never be blamed, as this desire to hurt her so deeply must be considered by others as God's will or a compulsion over which he has no control. But he knows it is not God's will or a compulsion over which he has no control because he also knows that he doesn't have to break her heart unless he wants to, and he discovers that it is impossible to do the things that would be a hurt to her just as long as he knows she is definitely in love with him. Therefore this knowledge that he will never be blamed by his wife for deliberately hurting her, who loves him dearly, makes it impossible to ever leave under these conditions, and this great security is assured to the wife just as long as she *shows* her husband that she truly loves him, for then only can his leaving her for any reason at all be a source of hurt. But when the husband is not conscious that the very words he uses in conversation is an indirect source of hurt to his wife, it doesn't take long before he destroys the desire on her part to show the love which is necessary for his security since the only thing that can hold her to him is his love for her; and when the husband sees that she doesn't love him he is unaware that the responsibility, in this entire instance, is his, and justifies what he does by blaming her. By making him conscious of this hurt that exists in words, she is permitted to continue showing her love, which makes it impossible for him to ever desire leaving when he knows she will never blame him for this real, not imaginary, hurt.

Obviously, therefore, this young husband, so much in love with his wife at this moment in his life, knows also that she will never desire to leave him as long as she knows he is in love with her. Consequently, since he knows that her desire to leave depends solely on him being out of love with her, which separation would break his own heart for which she cannot be blamed and he can prevent, he is compelled for his own security and happiness, completely beyond control but of his own free will, to prefer doing everything in his power to show that he is very much in love with her so that this desire to leave him for another will never arise in her. Both are compelled, under these conditions, to devote their lives to each other, doing everything in their power for the happiness of each, as that alternative considered better for themselves, because it is the only means by which they can prevent what they do not want, once it is understood that man's will is not free and what this means. This proves conclusively that God has given each individual the power of preventing the person truly loved from ever hurting him or her by revealing the mathematical corollary, the mathematical reason, why it is better for yourself when you don't blame. It also proves conclusively that any couple marrying under these conditions, regardless of how short a time they have known each other or for any other reason, must not only fall more and more in love with each passing year but must also find the greatest security imaginable without one ounce of obligation, simply because these increase with their passion and devotion. This is completely mathematical in every way and will not be denied when the rest of the relations are perceived. Because the husband and wife know they are under no obligation to each other in any way, sexual or otherwise, that they are free to come and go as they please, they will be compelled to control the desires of the other only by searching for what might possibly be a source of careless hurt for which they know they will never be blamed. If man's will was free this couple could leave each other regardless of the conditions that prevail, but they are absolutely incapable of desiring to leave, which proves again in a slightly different manner, that will is not free because not leaving is a motion, under these new conditions, in the direction of greater satisfaction and a preference for an alternative considered better for themselves, not better for the other person. This difference is one of extreme importance, which will reveal the reason for the conflict between parents and children. Are you beginning to see the difference between an opinion and a mathematical fact? By knowing that his own security with the person he loves depends on her love for him which he can control by showing his love for her, and by knowing that her own security with the person she loves depends on his love for her which she can control by showing her love for him, they are given no choice but to do everything in their power for each other as that alternative considered better for themselves. Consequently, any indication of selfishness, which word has never been adequately understood, only reveals the lack of love. In your present world, the words selfish and inconsiderate are used to describe the unwillingness to sacrifice a desire that does not hurt or involve the desire of the other person in any way. For example, if a husband should desire to get up from the dinner table before the meal is over to watch television or do something else, the wife considers this inconsiderate or selfish to leave her sitting there alone and blames him for this. But in actual, mathematical reality the wife, in this case, is the selfish one, for she is judging what is right for her husband, expects him to sacrifice a desire that makes him happy and does not hurt her in any real way, nor does he make any imposition on her desire to continue eating, which reveals that she is not in love with him for otherwise it would make her happy to see him deriving pleasure out of something that does not impose on her. If, on the other hand, his leaving was not an imaginary but a real hurt to his wife, he would be compelled to stay because the knowledge that she would never blame him for this hurt, and the realization that this hurt certainly does not show his love, which would only lessen his security, would make him prefer remaining at the dinner table.

Your incapacity to understand these mathematical, undeniable relations, which were revealed in the second chapter, may compel you to ask, "Wouldn't this allow a person to take advantage of not being blamed to do many things heretofore controlled by a nagging wife or a strong-armed husband?" Of course not, because taking advantage itself is a definite form of hurt which not only reveals the lack of love while lessening the security desired, but even if there was no love, it couldn't be done when it is recognized as a hurt for which there would be no criticism. Consequently, there is no advantage to take advantage under these conditions, for such a motion would be in the direction of dissatisfaction wholly impossible to prefer. However, many things do hurt in the life of a married couple only because they are in love, which could never hurt them otherwise. Again, there must be this line of demarcation between what is and what is not a hurt, which is drawn very simply.

If A has a desire which does not in any way make demands on the desire of B — otherwise it would be a judgment of what B's desire should be — then there is no way that B can exercise control over A, who is free to satisfy this desire. If, for example, a husband decides to play golf for the entire day, which does not ask that his wife do anything for him, yet his playing all day requires his use of their only car which she does not know how to drive, he is imposing on her desire to possibly use the car with someone else, which is a form of hurt. But he would know this immediately, and since he is anxious to show his love for his own security, he would be compelled to consider this possibility, for he knows that his wife would never blame him for taking the car and playing golf all week. Consequently, he is compelled to think things through very carefully before he speaks and acts because he doesn't want to reveal anything that would disclose a lack of love, since this would only encourage her to do the very things he doesn't want and for which he cannot hold her responsible. At the present time in your marriage, A blames B for a hurt which is A's responsibility. The husband blames the wife for making him a cuckold, when all the time it was something he could have prevented — providing he had known man's will is not free and what this means. But that's like saying Socrates could have ridden in an airplane or spoken on a phone, had these been available during his lifetime. Now the real problem of marriage centers on sexual relations, so observe how infinite wisdom (the perception of mathematical relations which belongs to all mankind) precludes every possibility of hurt.

If a husband desires to make love, which requires the desire of his wife, to pounce on her is an indication that he is not considering her desire. Or if she should ask him to have a relationship because she is in the mood, this again does not show a feeling of love because she knows that he will do anything to satisfy her, which means that she is taking advantage and therefore becomes impossible to do since this request only reveals her lack of respect for his desire. This means that by asking or pouncing the first blow is being struck by not knowing this is a form of hurt. By knowing, it is prevented with the knowledge that this hurt will not be blamed. By not knowing, it justifies the blame that follows and sets off a chain reaction of hurt, the responsibility for which is lost in the shuffle. To clarify this in another way I shall recall an experience I had with one of your psychologists who tried to prove me wrong by getting me to blame him for something he did, which only revealed to himself the extent of his unconscious ignorance and his incapacity to think with mathematical precision. I can still recall his embarrassment.

In trying to explain something to his colleague who could not seem to grasp these undeniable principles or relations, I finally decided to give it up as a lost cause, not only because his mind was obviously too confused with words to disentangle his thoughts, but also because I was getting very tired. It is taken for granted that some people will not be able to grasp these relations as easily as others, which is not a reflection against them, nor is it important, since they will learn the truth from the very fact that these principles work, which gives them no choice. A child will not understand this book at your present level, but he can be taught what it means that man's will is not free with actions as well as words. But this psychologist of whom I speak considered himself somewhat of an expert, and to people like him, it is an insult to their intelligence unless they can disagree. Seeing that his friend could not understand what he himself did not, he decided to take over the explanation for the sole purpose of ridiculing me. When I politely remarked, "If I needed your assistance, I would have asked for it," he responded immediately, "See, you're blaming me; you don't even live up to your own principles." To which I replied, "This only shows how little you understand of what I said, for if you had known that your taking over the explanation, even without the mockery, tacitly blamed me for stopping when I did, and that your obvious ridicule was an insult and a hurt, you would never have been able to do it had you known that I would never blame you for hurting me. Instead, you slap me in the face with an insult, blame me for not using good judgment, and then want me to turn the other cheek while excusing your conduct. However, under your conditions in the world of free will, you gave me complete justification to blame you since the corollary Thou Shall Not Blame only applies before something is done, not afterwards. When a man commits a murder or hurts another, it is only because you give him unconscious justification, but when he knows he will never be blamed by anybody for this terrible thing, it is mathematically impossible for him to derive any satisfaction because there is no way it can be justified, when every bit of tacit blame is removed. Your tacit criticism and ridicule were justified by a feeling of superiority, and only when this is removed, or only when you fully understand the principles in this book, will you lose the desire to judge someone else."

This is exactly what takes place in your present marriages. The husband or wife, by feeling superior, will criticize or judge what is right for the other person which strikes the first blow, and then when the other does not agree or conform, he is blamed. Consequently, if they both understand these mathematical relations, not only will the one be able to prevent any motion in the direction of retaliation, as was explained in the second chapter, but the other will be able to prevent any first blows from being struck, which allows your Great Transition to get under way.

It is important to understand that the solution to all the problems that exist on your planet is very interrelated, otherwise you will jump to a premature conclusion about certain things which will only be answered in later chapters. It should be obvious to your common sense that if a man and his family are starving for food the knowledge that you will not blame him for stealing a loaf of bread will not prevent him from trying to survive, for this is a motion in the direction of satisfaction. However, the very fact that he is starving only indicates that you have struck the first blow for which you want to be excused; but when you know that this terrible hurt to him will not be blamed, and when you are fully conscious of where the responsibility lies, you, my friends, will be given no choice. So instead of trying to judge this book in terms of your present mental development, try only to understand it.

Now sexual desire or passion is the true meaning of love, as was already demonstrated, and as was pointed out, when it decreases a marriage deteriorates. Consequently, once it is understood that you have the power to prevent adultery by revealing your love, it is obvious that the surest way to success is to arouse the sexual passion of the other since this demonstrates in an undeniable manner that you want your partner to be in love with you, which reveals that you don't want another mate since the love of your partner makes this an impossibility. By the same reasoning, as your mate makes efforts to arouse your desire, she reveals that she wants your love, which makes you conscious that she does not want another mate since your love for her makes this also a mathematical impossibility, as was just demonstrated. Consequently, when a husband and wife realize from the very beginning that the security of their marriage depends on arousing the sexual passion of the other without imposing one ounce of obligation, they are given no choice as to what is better for themselves since any action or word which decreases passion only reveals the lack of love by tacitly blaming the sexual desire of the other. This knowledge compels the desire to keep themselves in the same physical condition that first attracted their mate; otherwise, they will reveal that they do not love their mate which strikes the first blow and justifies adultery, since then infidelity could not really be a hurt to a person not in love, which releases B from the control of A. By obeying God's will, Thou Shall Not Blame, you are prevented from hurting yourself by preventing others from hurting you.

The stakes are very high here, and you can no longer be careless about your physical or sartorial appearance because you can no longer obligate your partner to remain under any conditions, but you will not want to be careless about anything because it will only deny you what you want. You were just confused. However, when a young couple gets married in your new world about to unfold, they are given no choice since they will understand all this and will know that any word or act that judges or blames another reveals a selfish desire that destroys the very security and sexual satisfaction desired. Consequently, when marriage begins on a mutual basis of sincere love (equal passion), and the principles in this book are understood, the very things that contribute to adultery are mathematically precluded.

This reveals that the person who has been obligating his partner to do anything, the one who tells the other what to do, how to act, how to speak, how to dress, where to go, what to do, is not in love, for these things decrease passion and are responsible for adultery. This same person finds it necessary to obligate the other to make love, and you wonder why there is so much adultery and divorce.

Two desires are involved, not one, and since it is impossible for either the husband or wife to approach the other (in the new world, of course) for physical contact, as this judges or tacitly blames, they are compelled to seek a means of arousing the desire of the other before any contact is made. This mathematically prevents them from ever taking each other for granted. If the girl is in the mood, she knows it is impossible to desire telling him that she wants to make love, for this imposes an obligation which decreases his desire while revealing her lack of love; nor can she approach to kiss him because this assumes that he wants to kiss her, and is a judgment that his desire is what she wants it to be. Likewise, it is impossible for this husband to desire pouncing on his wife just because she does not need an erection, for this does not consider her desire. How many times have you husbands and wives fondled each other in an effort to arouse desire, thinking that this was right? How many psychologists do you have who advised similar tactics, whose knowledge was justified by a Ph.D. degree? In reality, as our slide rule reveals, any time you lay a hand on your sexual partner without being absolutely certain this is what is desired, you are tacitly blaming a desire not to want what you want. If you ask a favor, you are tacitly blaming the possibility of being refused, which is a judgment that this other will desire to satisfy your desire. However, it is very easy to arouse the desire of the other for a sexual relation without physical contact at the beginning of a marriage, and very easy to continue this when the knowledge in this book is understood. All that is necessary is for them to keep their original appearance, allowing for pregnancies, and wear the kind of clothes around the house that stimulates the imagination and arouses desire, whenever the urge for a sexual relation hits them. For example, if a wife is in the mood all she has to do is put on a very sexy negligee, which conceals just enough to make him amorous. Then he knows what she desires, for she is plainly telling him, "Honey, I've got something for you — if you want it!" Remember, we are not discussing your present problems, which will be handled separately, although this knowledge will be applied once you are straightened out. The wife may even desire using certain words, for which she knows there will be no blame, since he knows she is not hurting him with them, as this kind of hurt is purely imaginary; otherwise, she would be prevented from using them by the knowledge that this hurt would never be blamed. Now, the moment he feels a twinge of desire or passion as a result of her efforts, which reveals her own desire, he never has to be worried about being refused or tacitly blaming her, since in this case she is extending a very warm invitation. This precludes, as in dating, any possibility of one partner ever desiring to punish the other by refusing. When a girl accepts a date, she is extending an invitation, and if she is not prepared to go all the way without contraception, she had better not accept. The wisdom here is amazing if you analyze it, and it is not mine.

During one of her menstrual periods, she doesn't have to explain to him; she just doesn't invite him to indulge his appetite. By the same reasoning, if the husband is in the mood, he must also don the kind of clothes to arouse her desire, which can also be done very easily. So many men have taken their wives for granted that it never dawned on them that they can also buy very sexy clothes to be worn around the house — translucent robes, jackets, etc., which will arouse their wives to accept this invitation. By obeying God's mathematical law from the very beginning of their marriage, this couple is compelled to keep each other constantly hot and bothered, and under these conditions, adultery and divorce are impossible, especially when all the other contributing factors are precluded. However, there is one change about to take place where sex and marriage are concerned that will absolutely amaze everybody on your planet and reveal in an infallible manner the great wisdom that directs every aspect of this universe, down to the smallest detail, for you are about to see why a husband and wife will never desire one bed for the two of them. That's right! Sleeping together, except as part of the sexual act, is about to take leave of your planet. Likewise is kissing, except as part of a sexual relation. This is not any different than other mathematical problems, and if you understand what it means that man's will is not free, and grasp what has been written thus far while having the ability to perceive and extend mathematical relations, you will easily see the solution. Now take note.

Since the person who prefers a double bed, without another bed available, is obligating the other to sleep together which action does not consider the possible desire of the other to sleep alone; and since the person who prefers a single bed, which means another bed is available, makes no imposition on the other to sleep together, it is obvious that whoever makes the decision for a double bed reveals an act of selfishness that demonstrates the lack of love (the lack of desire for passion in their marriage, for this is the only meaning of romantic love); and since neither desires to show what will only decrease the security of their marriage, they are given no choice. Further proof is the fact that the person desiring the double bed is actually blaming in advance the desire of the other to sleep alone, whereas the other does not blame by not making any demands. A's desire involves B, but B's desire does not involve A; it is that simple. This is completely mathematical, and if you study it over carefully, you will discover that man is given no choice in this matter of one or two beds. Once the true meaning of selfishness is clarified, once you know that all selfish acts, all acts that tacitly blame, decrease the very passion you want for a happy sexual relation, besides lessening the security of your marriage, are you given a choice? Visit us on Mars and see how we sleep.

As for kissing, except as a sexual act, it will also be wiped from the face of your planet because it is a judgment of what is right for another. How is it possible for me to walk over to kiss you unless I know you want this kiss? Who am I to judge that you desire to kiss me? If you should draw back because you don't like the smell of my breath, or for some other reason, I would be offended and blame you directly or indirectly since the approach itself is tacit blame; therefore, when I complain under these conditions that now exist because I don't like the way you acted, you are justified in striking back since I struck the first blow for which I don't want to be blamed. This tacit blame, which is an advance judgment of what is right for others, is at the very bottom of all the evil which came about out of mathematical necessity; but humorously enough everyone who previously made a speech or wrote a book about what he thought was wrong in human relations was right in the sense that he was obeying God's will, but now such an action would be wrong only because you know for yourselves what is mathematically right, which makes his opinions unnecessary.

How many times have you smothered your child with kisses to satisfy your desire, but what about the child? How many times did you kiss your wife goodbye in the morning only because you developed a habit, but how can you approach her now when you have the same conditions as with the double bed? Certainly, you can get in bed together. Certainly, you can kiss; but how is it possible to approach your wife before going to work, or for her to approach you, without judging that this is desired by the other? If she tells you that she wants to be kissed, then she is obligating you, which is not a sign of love; and if she asks you if you desire to kiss her, this is the same thing with an unconscious effort to shift the responsibility to you. The only thing she can do is wear something so sexy that you will be compelled to go the extreme with plenty of kisses before going to work, and if she is not in the mood, she had better not extend any invitation because she cannot check your desire, once she arouses it, without blaming you for what is her responsibility.

Now, when this young boy and girl complete their nuptials, which is, pure and simple, their first sexual relation, they will be very much in love. The boy will go home to his parents, the girl to hers, both dreaming impatiently of their next meeting, and they will know that there is no possibility of the other leaving just as long as they show their love, as was demonstrated.

It is not necessary that the boy or girl be working at the time because this marriage does not in any way impose an added burden on their parents, since they can continue living at their respective homes. If it did impose a burden, this couple would be prevented from getting married by the realization that the burden on their parents would never be blamed or criticized, which would make such a choice a motion in the direction of dissatisfaction. The only difference so far between a boy and girl going out on a date in your present world and between this newly married couple, is that the latter are permitted by the will of God to have sexual intercourse to their hearts' content, and prevented from hurting or leaving each other by the realization that this will only break the heart of the other for which there would be no blame. As a result of their indulging freely, they will be absolutely wild about each other in a very short while because of this unrestrained, uninhibited sexual passion, and no one will be standing in judgment over their actions because all your moralists will be silenced by the realization that they never knew the truth, only thought they knew — as your philosopher Socrates tried to tell you a few years back.

The boy knows, he doesn't have to be told, that when a child comes, it will be his responsibility, as the girl knows it will be her responsibility. He knows he is free to shirk this, to run away from earning a living, if he wants to, but he doesn't want to. He is also prevented from asking favors to help them financially when the baby arrives, because he knows that to judge what is right for others tacitly blames their desire in advance for not wanting to help. However, the friends and relatives of this couple, knowing that no favors will ever be asked, knowing that they will never be criticized for not helping, will desire, of their own *free will* (isn't this humorous?), to help when and wherever they can, without being obligated to do so by custom or convention since no one henceforth will judge what is right for another. Consequently, everything will be given, if desired, without being pressed by others and without expecting anything in return, not even to be thanked (for to expect thanks judges and tacitly blames what another should say), which compels this boy and girl to be overwhelmed with gratitude and to desire thanking everyone from the bottom of their hearts.

There will be no rush to get an apartment or home, but they will gauge this by her pregnancy and their desire for extreme privacy and convenience. There will be no possibility that they will go to live with either of their parents, first because they could never ask this favor, which tacitly blames in advance, and second because the parents could not ask for the same reason. Even if they were asked — is there something that could be done for them, they would be compelled to omit from their answer everything that can possibly be done by themselves because otherwise advantage would be taken of someone's generosity, which is no advantage under these conditions. Consequently the boy will make plans to support his wife and child for he realizes more than ever that he doesn't have to if he doesn't want to, that no one, no law, no parent, is compelling him to stay and support this girl; and this constant realization that not only his wife but nobody alive will ever in any way hold him responsible for leaving and breaking her heart, which he realized long before marriage took place, makes it impossible to hurt her.

She does not tell him to get a job or ask him when he is going to work; she gives him no advice whatever because she knows that such an action on her part would be a judgment of what is right for him which tacitly blames his own desire; besides, and still more important, it would reveal a lack of love which she wants to prevent since a display of affection, not with words but actions, is the only source of her own security. However, he will desire to go to work because the knowledge that this is the only way he can prevent the hurt to his wife and her parents who will never blame him, gives him no alternative. In most cases (when a baby is involved) it is the boy's responsibility to earn a living and handle all the money. However, since he is compelled to show his love, he is given absolutely no choice and will do everything in his power to make his wife extremely happy. This makes him figure out very carefully his entire expenses because he has no one to blame, and he knows that whatever he gives his wife she will never complain, never ask for one penny more. Since he must prefer doing everything in his power to make her happy, he will desire to give her all that he possibly can. This is his money, his labor, and he must make all the decisions as to how much goes here and there, but no matter how it is disbursed, he is mathematically compelled never to hurt his wife in the disbursement.

When it comes time to rent an apartment or buy a home, get furniture, etc., he will only tell her how much he can afford, and she will do all the rest, for this is her domain. He will be prevented from making any decisions where the house is concerned because this would be a judgment of what is right for her. In your present world the wife says, "Honey, where shall we put the television (this shifts the responsibility to him); would you like it over here?" "Frankly, I think it looks better over there, but you do what you think is best." In many cases the wife doesn't ask her husband for his opinion which he might unconsciously resent; or, if he is an interior decorator, he might not ask her for he feels that he knows much more than she does about decorating a house, which she might not resent because she believes that he does. However, wherever there is a difference of opinion, even if there is final agreement, there is an undercurrent of controlled resentment.

At dinner, she asks him what he would like, which tacitly blames his desire for something she might not be able to prepare. When the meal is over, he'll tell her it was delicious even if he didn't enjoy it, again developing this undercurrent of dissatisfaction which is only offset by the sexual relation.

After dinner, he may express his views about Russia or China or something else, and when she cannot keep up with this learned discussion, he feels like a genius, and she believes he is one. Should she disagree at this early stage he cannot afford to get angry as this would disrupt the fun they are planning to have in their double bed, so he will try, in a nice way, to show her where she is wrong. Just then, he may say, "Honey, would you mind going upstairs and getting my pipe and slippers?" "Of course not, darling," she answers pleasantly.

He will give her an allowance to run the house or his entire income, and before long, she tells him it isn't enough. "You'll just have to make more money." Little by little by little these little things that appear so insignificant get larger and larger and larger until, when sexual desire wanes, they will explode into arguments which destroy love all the more. Then, when he asks for his slippers, she says, "Gee, honey; I've got something else to do this minute; would you mind getting them yourself this time?" And he does mind. Before long he finds it difficult to get an erection, and by revealing her suspicion that she thinks he is playing around with another woman, he justifies doing that of which he is accused.

But when a couple in the new world moves into their home, the wife knows immediately that the house and the meals are her domain, while he knows that earning a living is his responsibility (this is just an example; they could have a different arrangement). Consequently, he never says a word about where anything should go because this would be a tacit judgment of what is right for her, and she never asks him because she knows he would always say, "It is up to you." However, because of this very fact, she is compelled to place everything in a position that she feels would be more convenient or comfortable for him, and regardless of what she does, she knows he will never criticize her decision. When a heavy piece of furniture needs to be moved, she doesn't say, "Honey, will you help me move this over here?" because this would be advance blame should he wish to refuse; but he, knowing that she will never ask him for a favor, asks her almost every day if there is anything he can do for her; and she, knowing that he would never blame her for taking advantage of his generous offer, is compelled to restrict her request to those things only which she cannot do for herself.

He doesn't ask her for his pipe and slippers, for this he can do for himself, and even if she had said, "Honey, is there anything I can get you?" he would have been compelled to reply, "Not a thing, dear."

You had no conception of how much ill will develops from just asking favors of one another, and in every case, it is the person asking, giving advice, telling others what to do, who is responsible for the disappointment and unhappiness that follows. By making a couple conscious of this responsibility for which all the world excuses them, they are given no choice but to change.

The husband doesn't express his opinions about what is wrong with the world, doesn't display his superiority, because for the very first time he realizes that nothing is wrong with the world, and that he is not in any way superior to his wife or anybody else, which you will understand better later on. There is no possibility for disagreement or discussion about two plus two equals four; consequently, there is no chance for an argument to arise. Assuming that the meals are her domain, he will never suggest as to what she should prepare. She, knowing that he would never criticize her should she make tasteless meals which would be impossible for her to do as this reveals a lack of love, is compelled to make a study of cooking long before marriage so that whatever she prepares he will look forward to eating; and she will rotate her meals in such a manner that he will be able to look forward to certain dishes according to the days, for looking ahead to something enjoyable is in itself an enjoyment.

Since earning a living is his domain (it wouldn't matter if the woman was the breadwinner, the same principle applies), she will never say a word to him about this, never suggest that he change jobs, never tell him that he is not earning enough money, for these are judgments of what is right for him; but he, knowing that she will never ask for anything, never complain about the money he gives her, is compelled of his own free will to do everything in his power to increase his income, but God will help him here with mathematical wisdom.

In the evening hours when they put on their sexy clothes — for under these conditions they will be compelled to desire each other tremendously — there will be a small atomic explosion of passion every time they are drawn irresistibly together, and even here they will study and learn the many ways they can have fun because once they are married there is no such thing as perversion, for it is a word with absolutely no significance. Everything goes and no holds are barred, unless it hurts the other person; but remember, most of the hurt you have been experiencing where sex is concerned is one of the imagination. However, what you desire may not be preferred by your partner, but in 100 percent of the cases, when a couple gets hot enough and all psychological impediments have been long since removed, their great heat or extreme passion will make everything they do enjoyable.

They will be able to satisfy all their personal desires just as well, without being questioned or criticized, but they will also be prevented from taking advantage of their freedom not only because this would display a lack of love which would lessen the security and sexual satisfaction desired, but also because it would definitely hurt the other person who is in love, and the knowledge that this hurt would never be blamed makes it impossible to derive satisfaction from taking advantage for there would be no advantage.

All the little standards that now exist and are responsible for innumerable arguments will be prevented from arising; and how this will be accomplished by those who now find in them such satisfaction due to an unconscious feeling of superiority, is marvelous to behold, as you will see.

You have standards for eating, dressing, color combinations, walking and talking. Ignorance is revealed by the very fact that your great hunger for knowledge and satisfaction compels you to swallow almost anything some writer or expert tells you, who is justified in what he writes because the publisher sees dollar bills in the ranks of his education, which stamps the brevet of truth on logical fallacies.

It is mathematically impossible for you to desire giving up what offers such satisfaction just because the standard judges what is right for someone else, which blames his desire to be different, but you will relinquish all standards except those that are completely mathematical, such as two plus two equals four, for two reasons. One, when you become conscious of how they hurt others, for which you will never be blamed; and two, when you realize how truly ignorant you are because of them, which then makes such a preference a motion in the direction of dissatisfaction. Just as long as you think the things you do and say reveal your superiority, you are given no choice, but what happens when, for the first time, in a mathematical, undeniable manner, you discover that the very things you felt revealed your superiority were only a definite sign of your genuine ignorance? Doesn't a man like Will Durant consider himself a genius because of his profound views on the entire world situation? But in actual reality, no book on philosophy could possibly get published on our planet simply because we all know the truth about our nature. Books like the Mansions and Story of Philosophy had great value in the world of free will, as did the Principles of Psychology by James, Freud's works, etc., but their value did not lie in the truth being revealed, only in the fact that it gave the writers and the readers an opportunity to move in the direction of greater satisfaction which helped develop the mind. These experts cannot be blamed for taking advantage of your ignorance and their own to earn a reputation and a living. How else could religion have been born, which takes advantage of your willingness to believe that God sits up in heaven answering your prayers? But remember — and this is the greatest humor imaginable — everything came about out of God's will. Your theologians reveal their ignorance, for which they cannot be blamed, by considering it blasphemous to show disrespect to a word like God, not realizing that this is only a symbol with no significance, which judges what is right for others and consequently makes their thunder of blasphemy blasphemous since it is unconscious disobedience of God's will, Thou Shall Not Blame, which unconsciousness makes it not blasphemous. Hey, God, tell them, am I being disrespectful? Are you beginning to see the great humor of your ignorance or is it still difficult to smile?

Why do you think your theologians advertise: "Those who pray together stay together," and why do you think your doctors advertise that a periodic checkup is important for your health, which is justified by the expression that "an ounce of prevention is worth a pound of cure?" It is for the same reason that any other advertising goes on — to increase business. But these doctors, priests, and rabbis cannot afford to be that honest with themselves; therefore, they are compelled to make you think it is for your benefit that they want these things, and they have come to believe it. What is more humorous than the speeches of a political campaign? Can't you see how tremendously happy these politicians would be if, at the very moment, they were telling you of how they are going to improve your lot, God thunders down and says: "Stop! Your speeches and promises are no longer necessary because the very things you politicians have been desiring to give the people I will perform as if by miracle," even though it puts all of them out of work. These politicians know the great humor of this political circus, but can you blame them for taking advantage of your ignorance as well as their own to get their names out in the limelight and pick up a rather easy way to earn a living... in comparison to the great insecurity of other ways? Can't you see that the very fact religion exists is a mathematical indication that your theologians unconsciously hoped that God would never become a reality, for he was being used to justify their manner of earning a living? Isn't it obvious that it is impossible to have faith or believe that two plus two equals four? If religion is founded on faith and a belief in God, what must happen when God is proven to be a mathematical reality? Is it humanly possible to continue having faith when you know that two plus two equals four? But remember, this is not a criticism because nobody is to blame for doing what he was compelled to do. Observe further how you were compelled to be dishonest with yourself.

When you tell your husband to wear a different tie with his suit you actually believe you are expressing your love for him, and are telling him for his good, but in reality, you are ashamed to be seen with him wearing a color combination that others will ridicule. Consequently, when the blame is removed you will discover that it doesn't make a bit of difference to you what he wears. Yet because this blanket of blame exists, and because you do not like when your husband argues with you over these things which you judge are better for him, you must justify it by employing a fallacious standard that gives the appearance of being true. Don't you agree that certain colors go together better than others? And you see this with your very eyes, right?

Now it should be mathematically clear to you at this point, with the exception of this difference in an imaginary superiority which will be clarified in the chapter on education, that all couples marrying under the conditions described, even without being married as you know the word, will be compelled to fall more and more in love through the years as each constantly represents for the other the satisfaction of enormous passion, which prevents any thought of adultery or divorce. In the final analysis, neither stays because it would hurt the other, for which there would be no blame, but because to leave would only be a terrible hurt to themselves. How is it humanly possible for either to desire giving up what is a tremendous source of satisfaction? Though this accounts for the future generations, for the boys and girls who are now approaching the age of nubility and understand what it means that man's will is not free, it does not take into consideration the hurt that presently exists in marriage and sex in general.

Many husbands and wives are in the process of committing adultery, getting or trying to get a divorce, and though this is not wrong — once the facts are understood since no one can blame them for preferring what offers greater satisfaction when the alternative is still worse — this, too, can be mathematically corrected by those who are unhappily involved, if they want to. Do you want to, you who are unhappily involved? Have I given you a choice?

To illustrate the great change about to take place even here, I shall add a little humor by taking an extreme case of a husband who has been trying in vain to get a divorce for the express purpose of marrying a single girl with whom he has fallen deeply in love. He has just finished reading the Inception of the Golden Age, which he doesn't completely understand, although he thinks he does, and is overjoyed to learn that he is now free to leave his wife since she will never blame or criticize his desire and since the laws too will henceforth be a thing of the past (this you will understand shortly). But he realizes that in order for him to freely leave his wife, she must understand this book, so it is imperative that he give it to her to read.

Because of innumerable arguments, he decided to get an apartment for himself, but was still supporting his family. How many husbands wish they could afford this luxury? So immediately after finishing the book he left his apartment with it under his arm to visit his wife. They had such a vehement argument two days ago that he wasn't sure of how she would receive his visit. But Harry was happy with this wonderful news.

"My problem is solved at last the very moment she reads this book," he reasoned prematurely, "for then she will never blame me for leaving her, never stand in the way any more of my getting a divorce." He is so happy that he can at last set himself free from this big fat sloppy nagging wife who every day would say, "Harry, where are you going, where have you been, why are you so late, why didn't you call, why didn't you come home for dinner; do this, don't do that, get me this, get me that," that he starts singing, "Happy days are here again, da . . da da . . da da . . da da . . . da da." As he knocks at the door, he is still humming when his wife answers.

What do you want, you little runt of a bastard?" in a sweet tone of voice; "what are you doing here, and what are you so happy about? You might as well forget about that divorce because I'll never let you marry that bitchy, no-good whore. If you think for one minute that you can ruin my life, make me miserable, and then expect me to help you find happiness with that cute little prostitute you picked up, you have another thought coming. When I die, that's when you'll get your freedom, you little squirt, so don't bother coming to see if I have changed my mind. You think I ever loved you? I hate your rotten guts. You were never any good. Now get out of here, but just remember to support the family if you don't want to go to jail, that's all. Go ahead, run over and live with that no-good bitch, whore, you deserve each other."

"Wait a minute, Becky, don't close the door; I didn't come over to ask that you give me a divorce; I know it is useless. I brought you something to read that I think you will find very interesting because you are a religious person who believes very much in God; isn't that right, Becky?"

"You know I believe in God, Harry; don't I go to church every Sunday with the children, and didn't I always ask you to join us, but you never did because you preferred to go bowling with the boys? How the neighbors used to talk."

Well, Becky, this author has positive proof that God is a reality, and he demonstrates in this book called Inception of the Golden Age how God comes down from heaven and ends all the evil in the world. In fact, this guy is direct from the planet Mars, and he says that no one is to blame for anything because God is responsible for everything."

"God is responsible!!!? What in the hell are you talking about? Do you mean that God is to blame for your committing adultery, for my not wanting to give you a divorce because you're a no-good rat, for my hating your rotten guts?"

"That's right! It's all right here in this book which I brought over for you to read. It's easy to understand, too. The theme is sort of a game; I won't blame you if you won't blame me. I won't blame you for not wanting to give me a divorce, and you won't blame me for wanting one. You know... tit for tat."

"Is that what the book is all about? After ruining my life, you don't want me to blame you because God is responsible, and now I should let you get off the hook, right? Isn't that what you want? No wonder you like this author, but you're both nuts. You can take that book and stick it up you know where. God is all goodness, and you, a rat born of the devil, want to blame our Lord for your running around with a slut, a no-good girl that would give her body to anybody."

"But wait, Becky, don't close the door yet; I'm not blaming God because I didn't have to do these things that hurt you so much, if I didn't want to, but God made me want to. You see, there was a purpose to all the evil, and therefore you shouldn't blame me for wanting to marry someone I love very much. I wouldn't blame you for wanting to leave me because I know God is truly responsible, and I don't even blame you for calling me all those names because I know you can't help yourself."

"Where in the hell did you pick up all that crap! That author must be a real goofball, but he's perfectly right about one thing. I am definitely not to blame because you are to blame, not God. That's right, you didn't have to eat my heart out like you did, hurt me to the core, hurt the children, ruin our lives; and I agree with you, you did it simply because you wanted to do it, and now I'm going to get even."

"Becky, I don't think you quite understand what I'm trying to explain, but I'm truly sorry about all that happened. I couldn't help falling in love with Mary, it was just one of those things ..."

" Yes, I know the very thing you are talking about, and I'm not blaming you either, but I can't help myself because God is making me make you suffer like you made me suffer. Now get out of here along with that other goofball from Mars."

"Wait one more minute, Becky; maybe I'm not explaining this book right, but everybody is talking about it as a fantastic mathematical revelation direct from the horse's mouth, God himself."

"Shame on you, Harry; how can you talk like that about our Lord... the horse's mouth!"

"Don't take me so literally, Becky. Anyway, this book is supposed to make everybody happy. Maybe it's a little over my head. However, it can't hurt you to read it, you might get some laughs, and you certainly don't have to agree with the guy if you don't want to, right?"

"I'll look it over, but not that it will change my mind about giving you a divorce. I agree it probably is slightly over your head because you never were too intelligent, and you never did get much of an education. My father used to tell me that you were absolutely nothing and that I was making a mistake, especially after my little sister beat you in a game of chess in twenty minutes. He could never see what I saw in you, and now I really wonder whatever possessed me to marry a squirt like you. Goodbye Idiot, and don't bother me again about a divorce."

Harry had accomplished his purpose, which was to give his wife the book to read, and he felt absolutely certain that she would never stand in his way once she understood that it wasn't right to blame him for wanting to leave her. He then phoned his girlfriend to break the good news, only to learn that she had already finished the book, but instead of being happy, she was somewhat perturbed and asked him to come right over.

"Harry, are you sure you understand this book? Do you fully realize what this means? This Martian has been throwing around a lot of mathematical relations, and some of them may have gone over your head."

"Certainly I understand, what's so difficult; that's why I'm so excited because I know my wife won't stand in the way of a divorce once she understands that this blames my wanting to leave, and she will never hold me responsible the moment she understands that man's will is not free."

"Harry, don't you realize that the very moment your wife accepts this knowledge, you are immediately divorced, as is everybody who is presently married, if you want to leave

Becky. You would be perfectly free to do whatever you think is better for yourself. You don't have to consult with the government or lawyers anymore. Now assuming that your wife and everybody else understands this book and stops judging what is right for another, which is this tacit blame he refers to before something actually happens, what are you going to do about supporting two families? How much money do you plan to give your wife and children for an income?"

"Whatever the law allows."

"But Harry (I sometimes wonder about you), once this book is understood by the entire world there will be no more laws, and assuming that this has already taken place, how is it possible to do what the laws dictate when there are no more laws?"

"I see what you mean."

"Consequently, it is entirely up to you what you give them since this must be your very own decision; I can't even help you out here. For that matter, you don't even have to give them a dime if you don't want to, and your wife and children would never blame you for this. Isn't that nice of them?"

"But if I gave them what has been the custom in such matters, they can get assistance from other sources, since many friends of my wife, her own mother and father, would help out; besides, if worse comes to worse, she can get assistance from the state... Oh, that's right, she can't because there's no more state; I forgot."

"Now you are beginning to understand, Harry. The laws and government, by judging what is right for others before something has even happened, are being removed. Therefore, your wife cannot get any financial assistance unless she asks her friends and relatives, but if she accepts the principles in this book, and knows that to ask favors of others blames them in advance for the possibility of being refused and disappointed, she will be helpless unless they come to her, and how do you know what financial obligations they might have. Everybody has their own problems. Furthermore, if you yourself grasped the fundamental principle, which is not to blame or judge another, how are you able to say what others should do for your wife. No, Harry; I'm afraid you are left completely alone to decide for yourself how much you will give your wife and family. How much do they get now?"

"Well, I earn $150 per week, have been keeping $10 for myself until I moved into the apartment, but now I need at the very least $50 just to exist."

"By cutting this income to your wife and children, Harry, do you think this has made it more difficult for them?"

"I'm sure it has, but what can I do, I don't have a choice. I just had to get away from that fat slob or else she would have driven me out of my mind. It's just like this guy Lessans says, it was the lesser of two evils."

"Harry, I can't tell you what to do with your money because you work for it, but let me point out that every penny you take away from what your family has grown accustomed to is a definite hurt to them, for which you will never be blamed; and remember, you don't have to give them a dime and you still won't be blamed or criticized, not even by me. Now, how are you going to support two families on $150 per week?"

"I have the solution, Mary; I didn't tell you before, but I've been offered another job paying $275 per week. However, I must go to Chicago for two weeks to take a training course."

"That's very good news; now all you have to decide is how much to give your wife and children of this income, and how much to give to us. Did you know that God has solved this problem for you as to how much money to give them, and though I don't want to judge your intelligence, you should be able to see this. Can you?"

"I'm afraid not, Mary; I'm beginning to think this guy is over my head."

"It is really very simple, Harry. If you have been giving your wife and family $140 per week at the time this book was understood by you, and this is the amount she has grown accustomed to, it is obvious that the only way you can reduce her income is when your income is reduced, which means that by giving her $139.99 you would be blaming her for receiving too much money. This doesn't mean you can't cut her income if you want to, Harry, because you can do anything you want to do, but you must bear in mind that whatever you take away from this accustomed amount is an increasing hurt for which you know your wife will never blame you, and when you know that she will consider your actions as God's will, though you know it is not God's will since you also know that you don't have to hurt her this way if you don't want to, are you given much of a choice? Certainly you are. All you have to do is decide how much you want to hurt them under these conditions, a dollar's worth, two dollars' worth, etc."

"Gosh, Mary, when you put it that way, it really doesn't give me much of a choice. But she really doesn't love me, that I know, so even if I gave her the entire $140, it wouldn't be too bad in view of this other job."

"But supposing you didn't have this other job, then what would you have done?"

"Gosh, Mary, I love you so much. I suppose we would just keep on seeing each other the way we have been until I could get an increase, or unless you continued to work until a baby came along."

"But supposing the baby came along, and you were unable to get a raise or a job paying enough to support two families, what then? Where could we turn for help? Remember, there is no more state, no more laws, no more asking others for favors. God is compelling us to shift for ourselves, so what is the solution, Harry, if someone other than yourself was unable to raise the money?"

"Thank God it isn't my problem because I don't know what I would do, frankly. Boy, am I glad that other job came along when it did! You see, God is looking out for little old Harry. Com'ere, Sweety; sit on little old Harry's lap and give him a great big juicy kiss... That was some delicious, honey, but you gave me a surprise; you don't have any pants on under your skirt, and now I could just love you to bits for you are def-in-ite-ly my precious, loveable, adorable, angel pie."

"Harry, should I put on my pants, or take off my skirt?"

"You know, honey, I do believe that Martian is right; man's will is not free, because you are not giving me much of a choice."

"What would you like to do to me, Harry?"

"Mary, we have an audience, and I'm afraid they would get too excited if I told them what I'm going to do to you. Your body is so gorgeous, baby doll, that I'm going to kiss you all over, starting at your little toe. I really love you, Mary, and proof of it is that I could never think of doing this to my wife, that big fat slob. I can't wait until you're all mine, forever and always. That's better, Mary, turn around into a more comfortable position."

"Harry, do you sincerely want to marry me?"

"More than anything else in this world. I could just kiss you... kiss you... and kiss you without ever getting tired, your body is so warm and passionate."

"There are two things that have me worried, Harry. The first is whether you are really going to be able to support two families, and the second, I'm not absolutely certain that your wife doesn't still love you in spite of everything. If she does, and is given an opportunity to show you her real feelings, do you think you could still come back to me?"

"You must be kidding, Mary. She hates my guts, and nothing in this world could ever keep me from coming back to you."

"Well in that case, Harry, you wouldn't mind going home for one solid week to satisfy my curiosity, would you?"

"This is really ridiculous, Mary, and frankly just a waste of precious time for we can get married right now; I want you to be my wife. But if it will make you happier, it's all right with me."

"I look at it this way. We have been making love for quite a while now, so one more week..."

"Three weeks, Mary. I'm leaving tomorrow night to get two weeks of training in Chicago and won't be able to see Becky until I get back."

"Well, so three more weeks won't make that much difference. Besides, even if you should change your mind, I'm really not that worried anymore about finding a husband since God has shown us the way at last. That book is going to set everybody's life in order, I feel it in my bones, even though I really don't understand everything. By the way, Harry, did you solve that problem with the alphabetical squares?"

"Are you kidding? I couldn't even understand the question. Anyway, I have enough problems of my own without wasting time on a child's game. Did you solve it?"

"I got up to five lines but could go no further. I don't believe that a child in the elementary grade is capable of working it out — Mars or anywhere else — and yet it is true we still play chess on Earth, and it is true we believed man had five senses and free will, and it is possible I could be wrong."

"Mary, that's enough talk about these other games; just turn back around and let us play the game we started when you interrupted me to get married."

"Well, since this might very well be the last time..."

"Don't say that, Mary; you know it is mathematically impossible, as that guy expresses himself, for me not to come back into your arms."

"Nevertheless Harry, to continue where you interrupted, since this might very well be the last time, and since you are going away for three weeks, and since we still have the entire evening to ourselves, you had better have your fill of fun because I know that it will be mathematically impossible, under these new conditions (assuming of course that everybody in Chicago has accepted these principles), for you to indulge with another. Take it easy, Harry, we have the whole evening."

When he returned from his trip, he approached his home with a certain amount of trepidation for he didn't know what to expect, although the rasping, critical voice of his wife still rang in his ears as he was about to knock. He really dreaded this week because he was absolutely starving for Mary, and though he thought the book would have some effect, never in a million years did he expect such a complete transformation as met his eyes when she answered the door.

After finishing the book and realizing that her husband was henceforth free to do whatever he thought was better for himself, Becky decided that it was better for herself to get back in shape. She went on a blitz diet, went daily to a weight-reducing salon, dyed her hair blonde, and bought some new clothes that revealed the charms that every woman has. She knew that if she wanted to get another man, she would have to make him want her, and she methodically planned to look her best so she could get married right away if someone came along who appealed to her. She knew that any number of men would like to go to bed with her, but under the new conditions, she was compelled to extend a flirtatious invitation only to the man she viewed as a husband. She, however, was not at all concerned about finding a husband since this new law came into effect.

When seeing her husband, she was quite surprised, but politely invited him to come in, and when Harry requested that he be allowed to stay at home for a week, she told him, without any questions about what was what with Mary, that this was his house as well as hers, and therefore her permission was not necessary. "Furthermore, Harry, I want you to know that I thought that book was wonderful, and that you will never be blamed or criticized by me again, regardless of what you decide to do, because I know that man's will is not free."

That evening, Becky prepared his favorite dinner: steak, mashed potatoes, fried onions, tossed salad, creamed broccoli, iced tea, and ice cream for dessert. He was never so satisfied in his life, and when dinner was over, he discovered that it was impossible to tell her to get him a thing in reply to her question, "Is there something I can get you, Harry?" But observe what Becky was compelled to do as a consequence of understanding the principles in this book.

She was very much in the mood for love since she had not indulged for quite a long time, and she knew that if she wanted Harry to make love to her, it was necessary to arouse his desire without touching him in any way. Frankly, she thought to herself, if Harry had not been there, perhaps she would soon be married to somebody else since his not being in love with her made it impossible for such an action to be a hurt to him, which made it possible for her to divorce him. By the same reasoning, Harry knew that if Becky showed him in actions, not words, that she really loved him, there would be no chance for him to leave, but there was only one way she could possibly do this. Consequently, a rather strange situation arose, for Becky was prepared to try everything to arouse his sexual passion so that her own desire could be satisfied, while Harry, remembering his promise to Mary, was determined to return to his love.

That evening, Becky put on the sexiest clothes imaginable and let him see just enough to whet his appetite, but Harry went to another room to get away from the temptation. The next night, however, while he was watching television, she stretched out on the sofa, let her dress slide up her thighs enough for him to glimpse what lay beyond, and then began to squirm in a very sexy motion. Finally, she asked him in the dirtiest language you use, "Harry, how would you like to...... and.... my little old...... Come on, Harry, take a good look baby; now tell me, wouldn't you like to........." Friends, this language is nothing; you should see what we use on Mars.

Well, Harry couldn't take it any longer, and when he finished making love to his wife, he was completely amazed at the degree of sexual passion and satisfaction that he experienced. By the end of the week, since there was no possibility for arguments to arise, their passion had increased since they remembered the pleasure and anticipated this renewed ecstasy. Harry realized that his wife truly loved him because she did everything in her power to arouse and then satisfy his sexual desire, without ever blaming anything he did, which meant that he could never leave her for another without seriously breaking her heart. It would be impossible for him to leave under these conditions because he would get no satisfaction hurting her this way. This is completely mathematical, and we shall now analyze it.

When this book is released and understood, every husband and wife will be standing on this moment of time called *here*, making preparation, so to speak, to move to the next spot called *there*. Consequently if two people have not been thinking about a divorce, and no matter how much they have been fighting and arguing, this knowledge mathematically prevents the one from any form of retaliation because it is impossible to strike back at the other under the conditions described and gone over several times, while it also prevents the other from doing the very things that under your present circumstances occasioned this desire to strike back.

If a husband or wife has been desiring to get a divorce but in vain, it must be remembered that every individual is completely free to do what he thinks is better for himself, without any fear from the laws, which only make matters worse now that the truth is understood. But this knowledge, instead of giving a husband his freedom, mathematically prevents it by compelling him to continue an income far above what the laws require, and secondly by making the wife or husband realize that the power to keep the person desired has been given to them. All that is necessary is to *show* your partner, in actions, not words, that you are truly in love. This means that you must try to get back in shape immediately, as did Becky, not for the benefit and happiness of your partner but for your own happiness and satisfaction. Then you must never touch your partner in any way until you have been aroused and offered an invitation. In other words, if a wife is in the mood for love, she can't hold her husband responsible when it is within her power to get him hot enough to come to her, and vice versa; but unless she does this, which requires a complete transformation of herself, he will be completely free to leave her for another woman since it is only her love for him that can prevent this great hurt to her; otherwise, it would not be a hurt. His knowledge that she will never blame him should he desire to stop supporting the family, that no one in the entire world will ever say a word of criticism, makes it impossible to derive any satisfaction or justification from doing so. Consequently, no wife need have any fear that her husband will hurt the family when he has this knowledge, but it must constantly be borne in mind that the word "hurt" where money is concerned is a reality, whereas with sex it is only so when you are striking the first blow for which you wish to be excused. By doing things that reduce the desire for a sexual relation, you are hurting your partner and demonstrating that you don't care, which gives ample justification to commit adultery since a warm, passionate sexual experience is the birthright of every individual. However, when all the things that gave this justification are removed, adultery is prevented, but this can only be accomplished if you want to. You can no longer turn to the laws, religion, or your experts in psychology and marriage counseling to try and get your partner to understand what should be done, because you are given no choice in this matter when you see the happiness that lies ahead once you obey God's will, Thou Shall Not Blame. But remember, this only applies before a blow is struck, not afterwards.

You are beginning to see the infinite wisdom that governs this universe when you remember that the laws and government are removed only because they are not needed at this stage in your development. By removing all forms of tacit blame, which is this judging in advance of what is right for others (habits that have developed over the years), and includes all forms of government, you are mathematically prevented from doing those very things for which government came into existence. There isn't any law that can compel a man to live with and support a woman if he makes up his mind that anything else is better. Consequently, when financial burdens increase along with a terrible feeling of insecurity, the slightest spark could set off a tremendous explosion of arguments which gave ample justification to shirk the responsibilities that were transferred to the government, friends, and relatives. Government does not come to an end because it is a form of blame, but only because it is a useless, costly appendage when the truth, which your philosophers have been searching for since time immemorial, is mathematically revealed. The services of a rabbi and priest during a marriage ceremony don't come to an end because they include the inculcation of a couple's obligations to each other, which is a form of tacit blame, but only because the boy and girl are getting married in a superior manner, which renders this service obsolete. Of what value is having a law that compels a man to pay alimony when he, of his own free will, will pay much more (providing this blanket of advance judgment, this blanket of tacit blame, is removed), or when he can never desire a divorce.

Think further about this immense wisdom. At the very time that God reveals what love is, a desire for sexual satisfaction which would allow a man or woman to fall in love with any number of people who can satisfy this passion, he prevents the possibility of having more than one sexual partner.

In your present world, the husband and wife blame each other because they are unconscious of who is really to blame. By revealing this knowledge that man's will is not free, which releases the corollary that no person is to blame, every individual becomes conscious that he alone is responsible for anything that is done to himself.

To make a successful transition in your marriage, all that is necessary is for both husband and wife to realize that the greatest happiness imaginable is compelled to result from obeying God's will, Thou Shall Not Blame, before something is done. If you want your mate, if you want a passionate sexual relationship, if you want real happiness, just obey the mathematical law of God; and if you do not want these things (remember, you are completely free to do what you want), just disobey this fantastic wisdom. Now, be perfectly honest with yourself. Has God given you a choice? Show me how free is your will by doing what you know will drive the person you want for sexual satisfaction away from your arms. My friends, it is a mathematical impossibility. You must constantly bear in mind that all forms of tacit blame notwithstanding have an inverse relation to love: the more you judge how your partner should be, the less you are in love, which judgment only decreases passion by striking the first blow while justifying a retaliatory measure not desired, just as fear itself tacitly blames, encourages, and justifies what is feared.

It should not be necessary to analyze every minute detail of marriage as this slide rule is applicable no matter what your marital problem is and enables you and those involved in your sexual life to solve your own. If you want your husband or wife never to leave you for another sexual partner, this is within your own power, providing you show your love, which means first getting yourself back into physical shape, and second getting your partner hot without physical contact. You can no longer obligate anybody, so if you want your partner to make love to you, don't be bashful, just extend a very warm invitation which includes remaking yourself. Remember, the very fact that you will never blame your husband for not supporting his family, even if he should stop giving you anything, will prevent him from desiring to hurt you and the children, so your problem where marriage is concerned is only sex. Obviously, the insecurity of earning a living has played hell with your lives, but you will soon behold a fantastic miracle because this insecurity is also coming to an end. It is only when all these loose ends are drawn together that you will be able to get a total view of this magnificent mathematical equation. So be patient and don't jump to any conclusions, as your geniuses are wont to do. All the facts will be in shortly. I know that it is hard to believe that government, religion, war, and crime will be wiped from the face of your planet, but so was it hard to believe many thousands of years ago the many other scientific achievements that are now in existence. Despite your opinion, the change about to take place is true because it is God's will; it is the mathematical direction man's motion is compelled to take, over which you have no control.

CHAPTER 5 — Children

Many years ago, your philosopher Plato dreamed of Utopia, but the only way he thought this could be accomplished was by removing the children from their parents at birth to prevent the passing along of ignorance from generation to generation. But this involved a gigantic assumption that his men of Gold, he himself and others like him who got the necessary education and had the ability to pass through the necessary steps, had already possession of what the end result should be and only needed the means to this end, such as a system to develop the men of Gold who would then remove the children from their parents for the purpose of controlling the environment, controlling completely what these little ones would experience. It never dawned on Plato and other philosophers that it was impossible for them to see the end result for this included the removal of themselves and their ideas which was constantly judging what was right for others; but what made matters still worse (not in reality of course since everything was necessary), what makes matters more difficult to straighten out, is the fact these men of Gold justified the veracity of their wisdom by being called men of Gold.

At every turn, I have observed on your planet that some people, perhaps you are one, think they are more qualified

117

to teach what is right and wrong because of some fallacious standard that justifies the thought by its logic. Let me clarify this.

The other day I happened to hear a rabbi criticize some journalist for his ridiculous column on the rearing of children, and to justify the criticism, it was revealed that this writer never even had a college education. This means that the worst kind of ignorance imaginable, the kind that really doesn't know but thinks so, is permitted to conceal itself in a logical relation which justifies its existence by assuming that the end result, as perceived by someone who has become a man of Gold, so to speak, is more valid. But the great humor lies in the fact that the end result, where children are concerned, has long been established in your thinking, and where you differ is not in what a child should become or develop into, but the best manner in which to accomplish this, which is exactly the thinking of Plato.

You do not question the necessity of an education, but what is the best manner in which to get children to want it. You do not question the necessity of teaching your children the difference between right and wrong, but you differ quite a bit on how to get children to obey what you think is right. What you know is better for your child is already taken for granted right from birth, just as it is impossible for the government not to take for granted the necessity of government. These thoughts are contained in the words and air you breathe.

Don't smile and think of someone to whom this applies because everybody on your planet is innocently guilty. The only difference is that a teacher will justify what is taught by assuming that his knowledge is reliable, whereas the others will justify what they say by quoting a teacher, a writer, a doctor, a priest, etc. One mother, in answer to my question as to what made her so certain she was teaching her children the right things, replied, "My doctor told me, and he's a very brilliant man." Another answered — her minister knows the difference between right and wrong and gave her explicit instructions directly from God. In every case, even when nothing but your own common sense is employed, there are hidden standards that justify the thought, which are completely fallacious, yet they guide your every move because of the tremendous amount of satisfaction derived from them. The rabbi was able to criticize the journalist because the standard he employed made him feel superior, but what would have happened if the same standard only revealed his ignorance? Would he have desired to reveal his ignorance to his congregation? Even the word doctor itself is an unconscious standard for it is a justification that symbolizes a logical assumption, and the fear that exists in the minds of people that they will only get worse if they do not consult this individual is the lever upon which unconscious ignorance further justifies its existence while being granted a legal right to hurt others with impunity, for which no one is to blame.

If this book were not a mathematical revelation which your scientists will be unable to deny, what do you think the clergy, the government, the medical, teaching profession and many others would do to what they would consider opinions detrimental to their security and power? They would pounce down with talons of steel and tear this book to shreds. But though they and others will be dissatisfied to learn the truth when it deprives them of such tremendous satisfaction, they are compelled to be silent because to utter any words in protest would only reveal their great ignorance, which can give them absolutely no satisfaction, giving them no choice. No child likes to have their toys taken away, but if they are hurting others, then something must be done. However, just to announce that man's will is not free isn't sufficient to make the world leaders, those who are constantly judging what is right for others, give up what to them is a source of satisfaction. How was it possible for Plato to give up the notion that he was wrong when he saw that he was right? Is it possible for socialism and communism to relinquish the thought that they are right when they think they are not wrong? Is it possible for the leaders of capitalism to resign from their jobs when they think their services are required? It is, as always, this taking for granted that the end is true, that which you think is true.

For example, even a person like your philosopher Will Durant takes for granted certain truths in bringing up a child, and what he considers wisdom makes no reference to any change in the end itself, but only to certain techniques in the means to accomplish this end. He believes that certain foods are more wholesome than others, that a child of ten should be in bed at an early hour and consequently considers it wisdom if he can get his child to eat what he thinks is better, get her in bed at an hour which he thinks is better, play the kind of instrument and music he thinks is better for her, etc. A person like Durant does more harm to a child because of his successful means than a father who fails with his invectives and commands. Let us follow this philosopher for a while as a basis to demonstrate the source of this unconscious ignorance.

Rule number one with him is air. "Every night, whatever the season may be, open windows call in the wind to turn the cheeks of Ethel into roses and flame." He places great emphasis on rosy cheeks which teaches his daughter that "whatever the season may be, open windows to call in the wind," is of great value. Now, just supposing this child had a physical condition which became aggravated by a cold inhalation during sleep, but which would never have developed into anything serious if she were allowed to move in the direction that was better for herself. Her own nature would have made her uncomfortable during the night, and she would have gotten up to close the window even at the sacrifice of rosy cheeks. But being made to believe that her father is a genius who knows all the answers as to what is right and wrong, she would desire sacrificing what is truly better for herself, providing she discovered an aversion to keeping the windows wide open in the middle of winter, in favor of her father's desire. If he conveyed the thought that he really doesn't know what is better for her, but he preferred for himself wide open windows, then at least she would be in a position to judge for herself what is more comfortable. Under his conditions, she could really get sick since he is judging what her body requires, which then would necessitate calling in a doctor who would literally guess at the trouble, prescribe some medicine to satisfy her fears, and end up by making matters altogether worse.

Included in rule number one is the time he believes his daughter should be in bed. "Many a bribe of tender words, and dimpled arms around the neck, has been offered us for permission to 'stay up' beyond the year's decreed retiring time. But here we have been quietly and inconspicuously resolute; we will not condescend even to discuss so absurd a proposal; we turn it aside as a criminal idea, and send Ethel up to Morpheus every evening at her usual hour. Now, though she is a great lady of almost ten years, she still disappears regularly at eight-fifteen, wishes us from the staircase 'tight sleep and pleasant dreams,' and is all tucked in and set by half-past eight. The law has been broken now and then, as when some genius of the piano was honoring our home; but for the most part it has been with us a sacred monastic rule, a trifle of surpassing moment in our philosophy."

It is obvious that if he had known man's will is not free and what this means, he would never have been able to judge what the desire of his daughter should be; consequently, he was not concerned with her judgment about what was better for her, only about his judgment. He was not aware that every time he opposes her desire, her entire body is unhappy which makes her vulnerable to sickness of some sort, even the kind that is feigned. In comparison to this father who says, "Ethel, get the hell upstairs to bed right now, before I spank your little tail," Durant considers his means an expression of wisdom. But why should he make such an issue of the time; what difference does it really make if the child was happier going to bed when completely exhausted from having fun? He takes for granted that the knowledge which guides his actions towards his daughter is correct and never questions it. Isn't it obvious that she would have been much happier to stay downstairs; but he was not concerned with her happiness when it contravened principles which he held true. He believed that there was some truth in the expression, "Early to bed and early to rise," and some truth in how many hours a child of a certain age requires. Besides, he wanted her to be rested for school so she would accomplish her work in a more healthful manner. Yet, though he was not doing what was healthier for her, he thought he was, just by the fact that he considered himself a genius, which justified the thought. Proof of this is the fact that God states explicitly — Thou Shall Not Blame, and he definitely blamed the desire of his daughter to stay awake. "But," you might ask, "how is it possible not to criticize, judge, or blame some desires that children have?" The question itself reveals your ignorance, so be patient and you will soon have your answers.

Rule number two in the philosophy of this individual is food. "We found that Ethel flourished on a vegetarian diet helped out with plenty of milk and whole wheat bread; she grew tall and strong, athletic and alert; and it seemed to us that she was getting every element needed for full development. But the vegetarians will be scandalized to hear that very soon in Ethel's history we added chicken to her menu once or twice a week. We call her a 'chicken vegetarian'; and on that queer unprincipled diet this little household has been prospering physically for a decade. Ethel's health-record is not perfect: she encountered German measles in her infancy, but outlaughed it in a week;

at four she caught whooping cough from a playmate, and beat it down with the help of the new serum; at eight she developed swollen tonsils, whereupon they were removed. These are the blots on her 'scutcheon,' otherwise she is a stranger to doctors and disease. 'How does it feel to have a stomach-ache?' she wants to know."

Although it is true that she could not express a desire for a different kind of food when not given a choice, while being in good health, Durant once again put the cart before the horse by assuming that her physical condition was directly due to what she ate. Had this child been allowed to choose between various meats, poultry, fish, as well as a large variety of vegetables, or had the meals included this larger variety, she might have been a much happier person. By restricting her to whole wheat bread, milk and a chicken vegetarian diet, he once again assumed what her body required. By removing her tonsils, he relied on the advice of a doctor, but in actual reality, if man had something removed every time it became infected or swollen, he wouldn't have much left. This does not mean that no tonsils should ever be removed, but where is this mathematical line of demarcation when a doctor is dependent on this removal to earn a living? This operation is justified on the grounds that the tonsils are a vestigial organ which serves no purpose now, but are the doctors who remove them absolutely certain they do not serve a useful function? We will put doctors to a little test later on.

Durant doesn't discuss the problems that some people have in trying to get their child to eat foods considered better and more wholesome. Most people threaten the child with some form of punishment unless he eats the quantity and quality of food the parents mistakenly believe are necessary, but our philosopher never had this as a personal problem.

Rule number three is play, according to Durant, who judges constantly what is better, "and taking all these growing muscles, senses and limbs, teaches them coordination, precision, unity. The perfect parent," since he appears to know he must be one, "would have, as an element in his artistry, a knowledge of just what toys to buy to encourage the development of every organ and every power." He is not interested in finding out what the child prefers to develop, only what he thinks should be developed. He is constantly judging what is right for others, the very opposite of what God's mathematical corollary reveals to be undeniably true. He was compelled to believe in free will in order to justify his constant criticism and judgment of others; how else could the Story and Mansions of Philosophy have been written? How was it possible for the Ten Commandments to come into existence unless religion believed in free will?

His moral instructions are: "First, use the word don't sparingly," not because this is an unconscious perception that no one can be blamed, but only because he recognizes that this would only hinder the accomplishment of what you desire for your child. "Don'ts are necessary, but every parent should be restricted to a limited number of them, like a doctor with alcoholic prescriptions; and perhaps, like the doctor, he should exhaust his annual allotment on January first."

Since it was impossible to get his daughter up to bed every night at the time he decreed without exercising a form of don't, he was permitted to use this alcoholic prescription, which her dimpled arms about his neck could not change.

Because he methodically aroused her desire to play the piano, he actually believed he was giving her a choice, and when she lost interest, he again employed a psychological technique not to satisfy her desire, but his own. He was so successful in this regard that if she could have ended up a happy lover of Elvis Presley, rock and roll, and the saxophone — had he left her completely alone — his technique would have gotten her to sacrifice this happiness in favor of what made him happy. In his mind the piano and classical music was what he wanted his daughter to play; simplified selections from Beethoven, Mozart, Schumann, Schubert, Handel, Haydn and Bach; he was not interested in any other musical instrument, nor in rock and roll. Consequently, he never gave her a choice among the different types of music but aroused her desire by speaking of certain aspects until she felt like learning how to play, and then he left it up to her choice, which was no choice since she was obeying his will not her own.

Durant is not one ounce different than other fathers trying to impose their will, except in the means to attain this end. He is so confused with words that he says, "Perhaps, too, we can substitute praise for blame in forming the character of the child," not realizing that whatever is praised is an inverted form of blame, which justifies not doing what is praised when the praise is not forthcoming. He gives his daughter a monthly salary "dependent upon her keeping her room tidy, making her own bed, getting up promptly, arriving at school on time, and doing her lessons well," which obviously blames her for not doing these things. He says, "Censure cramps the soul, and makes the imperfect task forever hateful; praise expands every cell, energizes every organ, and makes even the most difficult undertaking an adventure and a victory," which plainly tells us that praise is so powerful as a means to an end that you can get a child to do what is not liked, perhaps even hated, to earn the praise. "Egotism is the lever by which we can move the world" to do the bidding of others without using force, which only changes the means, not the end. "Instead of pouncing upon work ill done and heaping up reproaches, we keep an eye alert for things done well and mark it with praise that shall linger sweet in the memory as a call to further accomplishment," for the purpose of accomplishing what the parents want, not what the child desires. "If Ethel has to report she has fallen short in arithmetic, we show regret, but we have not the heart to reprove her," as if showing regret is not reproof, which demonstrates how confused this man is with words. "But when she comes home with news of perfect marks we dance and celebrate, and exhaust our ingenuity to show new joy at each victory." But supposing he is tired one day and doesn't feel like dancing, what then? "When she has done something that especially delights us we have slipped a dollar into her bank," and a seal, for a good performance, is given fish. And what would he do if his daughter especially, especially, especially delighted him? Isn't it obvious that she is performing to get paid, just like a man working at a job he doesn't like but stays because of the money.

Since he gives her a monthly salary dependent on her doing certain things, and not to give her this monthly salary would certainly be a form of punishment which he doesn't approve of because he writes, "It is remarkable how well behaved a child can be without punishments and without commands," he is compelled to resort to pride in addition to praise in order to prevent Ethel from desiring not to do that for which she is being paid, so that he doesn't have to stop her salary which would be a form of punishment. "We suggest to Ethel that she is too proud to let anyone see her untidy or unclean; that she is too proud to run forward for gifts or preferment; too proud to let anyone surpass her considerably in her work." Each thing reveals the standards which govern his every thought, and that he is a part and parcel of his time, except for the means.

But he does believe in the worst form of punishment imaginable, although he is not conscious that it is the worst, when he lets "her see how her defection from honor has darkened the day for all." He makes her conscious that she has committed a terrible crime which hurt her father and mother very much, who refuse to blame her despite this. This is cruelty personified because the parents were not hurt, and it compels the sacrifice of a great part of happiness to satisfy the selfish desire of another. It is equivalent to a father taking advantage of a child who loves him to ask for a glass of water. If the child refuses because this service would entail interrupting something giving the child pleasure, the father, employing his psychological technique, would then say, "That's all right, honey, you don't have to get it for dad if you don't want to." The child, being made to feel guilty, suddenly desires very strongly to do what was asked because she is conscious of hurting her father, who is not blaming her for this.

The important question, however, is not this means, but an end never considered before, because certain facts about your nature were never understood. The question is not what is the ideal time for children to go to bed, but why is this important; not what is better, communism, socialism, or capitalism, but why is government needed at all?

Now the entire problem of raising children in the best possible manner is easily solved the very moment you apply the mathematical slide rule, Thou Shall Not Blame, because then you are made conscious of the fact that only one road is open for travel. Since you can't blame a child for anything he desires to do, it is obvious that you must prevent certain desires, the ones you consider harmful in some way, from arising. Consequently, from the very first day, it is important for the parents to determine only what they feel would be a real, not imaginary, hurt to either their child or themselves, for which the baby, now and all through life, cannot be held responsible. But if they are unable to prevent (take note of this mathematical wisdom) their child from desiring what they feel will be a hurt, or prevent their child from not wanting what they think will be for his benefit (both without any form of blame), it is rather obvious that what they like or dislike — and cannot prevent without blame — is something not in any way harmful to the child and exists only as an imaginary fear based upon false knowledge, otherwise they would definitely have the power to prevent this harm without blame in any form. Do you realize what this means? For the first time, you are going to see how dishonest you have been compelled to be with yourselves and your children.

If, for example, Durant perceived some great benefit to his daughter being in bed at eight-fifteen, then there is only one thing he can do in order not to blame her desire to stay up past that time, and that is develop a habit whereby the entire family retires at that time; but even then, he can never be assured that she may not desire to stay awake longer, either reading, watching television, or doing something else. But this kind of means already involves his desire, and what about if he doesn't feel like going to bed that early to set the example? If it meant that Durant would have to sacrifice hours on his books because of this imaginary harm, he would be given no choice, but God is giving him a choice: either let the child satisfy her own desire or sacrifice his to develop this habit.

If not eating spinach is harmful to the child then the parents will be compelled to discover a way to prepare it so that he can like it the very first time it is tasted, for persuasion in any form (which includes all efforts to arouse some desire toward a particular end, as Durant did with the piano but especially after the desire of the child has already been expressed) can no more be used as it is a method of blame and an assumption of what is right for the child. But if they cannot prevent him from disliking the spinach no matter how it is prepared, or from liking rock and roll instead of Beethoven (without any form of blame), it is obvious that the harm they perceive has existence only as a figment or improper relation of their mental development.

This makes it absolutely impossible for a person to be careless anymore where children are concerned, because the moment a mother realizes that she cannot judge what is right for her children unless it is without blame in any form, she is compelled to think like never before in order to avoid starting a habit she has no way of stopping without blame, criticism and punishment.

But the problems that presently exist will not be placed in the same category as those confronting a couple with a brand-new baby. First, we shall take care of the latter, then the former; and as we proceed, we shall shed by the wayside a number of false beliefs or opinions by following the basic principle.

The first and most important thing to remember is that a child has his own desire, and under no circumstances can his desire be criticized, blamed or punished for anything. Consequently, as is the case where sex is concerned, you cannot do anything to this baby or child unless you know this is what the child wants; otherwise, you are blaming his desire. Therefore, to assume that this baby prefers or desires some form of canned or desiccated milk, rather than his mother's breast, is a judgment of what is right for this baby. Since the breasts are put there for that purpose, the only thing that could possibly make a mother prefer not using them to feed her child is the advice of a doctor who will tell the mother that it doesn't make any difference; but it does make a difference to the child. It would be time enough to prepare some formula if the child refused his mother's breast, or the child was not thriving, but not until then, because otherwise you are blaming this child's desire.

Durant writes: "In the first three months we were guilty of a grave blunder, for we allowed our child to be used as a laboratory for a newfangled form of desiccated milk. It is a crime which many years of parental solicitude cannot quite clear from our memories. We believe now, with Ben Franklin, that the human race should beware of young doctors and old bachelors," as well as all philosophers and everyone else who expresses only opinions.

Now when a baby cries, it is usually for one of several reasons. He is hungry, dirty, and uncomfortable, in pain or just spoiled, which is a word to describe a habit, not good or bad, the parents allow to develop in the child who is then blamed for some annoyance. Consequently, if he is fed, kept clean, comfortable, and not spoiled, the only thing that could make him cry would be pain. However, when he discovers that his cries result in being picked up, he will cry for this reason, so if this is a source of annoyance to have to rock the baby to sleep, pace the floor at odd hours of the night as the lesser of two evils, then you had better never develop this relation.

Quite often, visitors will pick up a crying baby without knowing that this develops a habit which is a great annoyance to the parents who are left with the responsibility of breaking it. But now these people will be prevented from this by the realization that they will never be blamed for this concrete hurt. Consequently, everyone will be compelled to desire picking up a baby only when he is not crying.

The next thing proven completely false by our slide rule is the waking of a child or adult for anything at all, since this obviously blames the desire to sleep. Remember, when someone is asleep, he desires this, and for him to be awakened by a doctor or anybody unless his sleeping is obviously harmful (such as a fire which would reveal his desire to be awakened), you are imposing your desire and judging what is right for him. This offers conclusive evidence that any fears a doctor may impart regarding the necessity of waking a child to administer medicine or for a feeding, examination, or anything you care to throw in are completely unfounded and grounded in unconscious ignorance. When a doctor advises these things, it is only because you are asking for some advice, which he takes advantage of to earn a living, for which he cannot be blamed.

It should be obvious that the only way you can get your children out of bed without blame is to teach them how to use an alarm clock. Then, if they desire to get up at a specific time, if they desire to go to school, they will, and if they desire to sleep, there is nothing you can do about it unless you blame them. Furthermore, if you can't prevent this desire to stay home from school without blaming the child, then it is mathematically obvious that the harm you perceive by not getting an education as you know it is purely imaginary — once the blanket of blame is removed. The very fact that the educational system was never held responsible for children hating school compelled the parents to force their children, one way or another, which increased the business of the doctors just from the feigning of illness these children preferred as the lesser of two evils. But when parents and teachers are compelled to withhold their judgment as to what is right for the children, which allows these boys and girls to stay home from school if they want to, the educational system is forced to change in a drastic manner so the children will desire to go of their own free will, otherwise the schools will go out of business — as you know the schools.

As for bedtime, this again is not your business. The child knows what time he wants to get up, and if he knows he has to be at a certain place at a certain time — otherwise this will be a hurt to you for which he knows you will never blame him — he will be there; but if a child doesn't want to go to school, who is being hurt? How is your child hurting you by staying awake as long as he likes unless his presence annoys you in some way? What difference does it really make to Durant if his daughter stays awake having a lot of fun, and then falls asleep from sheer exhaustion? Think of how happy the children would be if there were no restrictions as to their bedtime. Most of you, like Durant, have come to believe that children should be in bed at a certain time, which only reveals your ignorance when all the facts are understood. Naturally, when a child oversleeps, gets to school late, is punished by the teacher and parents, it is obvious that he made a mistake by sleeping late, just as it is obvious that he makes a mistake when not finishing high school or college since everybody judges him by certain standards; but when these standards are removed it can be seen that the fears of the parents and children were not directed towards the lack of an education, but to this judgment of their inferiority. You are in for quite a lot of surprises.

Remember, there is nothing wrong with wanting your child to get in bed at a specific time and if you can do it without blaming the desire of this child in any way more power to you, for no one will ever tell you what is right for yourself; and the only thing that will make you prefer not blaming your children in any way will be the realization that this will result in your complete happiness as a family unit. Every argument that exists between parents and children arises from ignorance, for which the parents are innocently responsible. Once they are shown what is truly better for themselves, they are given no choice, so pay careful attention to what follows and see if it is mathematically possible to deny the knowledge to be revealed.

Now it is obvious that when a child begins to crawl he cannot be blamed for desiring to climb on furniture, yet many of you do blame this baby by saying, "don't," "naw naw," "musn't," "don't touch," "stop," "hold it," or you will just pick up the baby every time he is about to touch or climb on something you'd rather he stayed away from. But no matter what words you use, no matter how you check his desire, you are blaming him. Consequently, since our mathematical corollary reveals that man is not to blame, you are given only one possibility: you must prevent the desire of this child to climb on furniture from ever arising. This necessitates keeping him in a playroom, play yard, or playpen, where nothing will check his desire in any way. At the same time, you are compelled to remove everything that might possibly hurt this baby because the knowledge that your husband or wife will never blame you for this hurt, when you know it is definitely your responsibility, gives you no satisfaction. This constant knowledge that you will never be blamed by anyone for any careless hurt to your child, compels you to think like you never thought before, because there is no satisfaction in being excused for something that could have been prevented when there is no way it can be justified.

By the time your child learns to walk, he will have learned the difference, without being taught, between furniture and toys, living quarters and play quarters. Then he will never desire to play in the wrong part of the house without ever having to be told; but by constantly telling a child not to do this, don't do that, stay away from here, etc., you only give the child ample justification to do, sooner or later, the very things for which he was blamed. Furthermore, every time you check his desire, you strike a first blow, and before long, he will get satisfaction in striking back at you. When your back is turned, he will do the things you don't want, and when visiting friends, he will embarrass you by jumping on their furniture. So take note now, in order to prevent the very things you do not want all that is necessary is to obey God's will — Thou Shall Not Blame — which compels you to keep a child always in a playroom, play yard, or playpen until he begins to walk so that there is no possibility of checking his desire in any way, and so that when he is allowed to enter the other living quarters there will be no possibility that he will desire to climb on furniture or knock anything over. Remember, under no circumstances can this child be blamed for anything because everything he does is your responsibility, for which no one will ever blame you.

In the world of free will, you were often careless, and when a child got hurt, you blamed your partner for being so negligent. This blanket of blame justified the carelessness because you could always defend yourself with an excuse or extenuating circumstance. But when this blanket of blame is removed, and you know that whatever you carelessly do that hurts your child will never be blamed, even if the child should die — because it is impossible to hold someone responsible for doing what he is compelled to do — it becomes impossible for you to derive any satisfaction from being excused for what you know you could have prevented if you were not careless. Consequently, a man will remove all his razor blades so that there will be no possibility of a child getting hurt with them, because he can think of nothing that offers greater dissatisfaction than that he should be directly responsible for hurting someone when there is no possible way he can excuse it. This compels both husband and wife to think like they have never thought before, which prevents all mankind from making mistakes. However, it is necessary to point out the various ways children are hurt, and the ways in which children are made to hurt their parents who have been blaming them for what is their own responsibility. Consequently, since the parents do not like to disappoint a child who asks for things and favors which they cannot always give without annoying or hurting themselves in some way, they are compelled to prevent, without blame, a child from ever asking for this or that, just as if they knew what it means that will is not free. Also cleared up with one simple stroke of God's magic elixir is jealousy among children, envy, possessiveness, selfishness, arguing, fighting, and all the other things that disturb and annoy the parents. Wouldn't it be wonderful to get rid of all these things that cause such a disturbance and make your living so much less enjoyable? Are you given a choice? But mind you, it is demonstrated that these things will take leave of your planet not because they are worse for the children, but because they are definitely a source of dissatisfaction and unhappiness for the parents.

The problem is solved first by the very fact that the children born to parents who have married under the optimum conditions described will never hear an argument or raised voice, never hear a request for a favor, never hear one parent blame the other, and consequently, no words or expressions will develop with which to do these things. Children imitate; even your present psychologists will confirm this, which is the reason why Russian children speak Russian, Chinese children speak Chinese, etc. If a child does not hear a request for a favor or is not asked to do one, how is it possible for him to imitate what never becomes part of his mental development? Asking for a favor or asking for anything that is not preceded by, "Is there anything I can do for you?" would have as much meaning for a child as this word BGHCA has for you. Besides, at a very early age, children can be taught what it means that man's will is not free, which will automatically prevent them from extending any word relations that tacitly blame another. Consequently, up until that time, the manner in which children get what the parents and others have to give plays a vital role.

Durant, by dancing for joy at his daughter's good marks, is giving her a certain amount of entertainment, which develops a habit that encourages her to study hard to get these real good marks in order to watch her father dance with joy, but supposing he doesn't feel like dancing, what then? The child is disappointed, which blames her father and justifies not getting any more good marks. One father started out by giving a child a penny for this, a nickel for that, and a dollar when getting this and that together. Soon, he was paying out more than he could afford, and how was it possible to stop without disappointing and blaming the child. Furthermore, what is given influences the child to do what is really not desired because of some intrinsic value to him, which makes him stop working when not paid. And what about the many things that parents give which involve their own desire, such as dancing for joy, or taking a child somewhere in the car, or getting down on their hands and knees to play with him, even when they are not in the mood, just because he expects this, and it is either disappointing him or tiring them out. If you disappoint children, even with an explanation, they resent it, which you can only compensate by renewing your promise for another time. Before long, you are under a tremendous obligation to your children to do many things you really don't want to do. However, this problem is very easily solved by giving the children absolutely no gift directly, and nothing in payment for something else, for the latter imposes an obligation while the former develops a habit of expectation which is often followed by disappointment, associates the giver with the gift, encourages partiality, and makes them possessive, which engenders envy and jealousy. Therefore, when a child expects what you cannot always give (which is a source of disappointment), shows partiality and becomes possessive, you are compelled to blame for being so annoyed in order to correct what could have been prevented by not giving gifts directly. If you prefer such annoying actions, that is your business for which you will never be blamed, but how is it humanly possible to prefer what can only be a source of unhappiness where everyone is concerned, since the children will always expect more than can be given.

By the same reasoning, no praise or compliments are given to a child for anything at all because this places a fallacious value on what is being done, which must be desired for itself. Everything Durant did was to place a fallacious value on what existed for his daughter. She didn't go to school because she liked it but because he liked it for her, and he was willing to pay her a reasonable price to satisfy him, just as an animal is fed something to eat for a performance. I know a child who literally hates school, but I'm willing to bet that he has his price. However, if you stop paying there is nothing in school itself to make him desire continuing.

Now remember, if you want to give a child toys he must never know whence they came because this will only develop a partiality relation, and if this is one of the conditions under which you buy presents for children it is obvious that the gift is primarily for your benefit, not that of the children. By giving a gift directly, it is obvious that you expect a certain amount of thanks and appreciation for what you have done, which blames the receiver, when old enough, for not reacting as you expect. When a boy and girl receive gifts after getting married, as described, the conditions change because this couple knows that man's will is not free and what this means, which prevents any partial relation from developing, but not so with a child. Consequently toys are placed in a child's room, but if there is more than one child who are not old enough to know the value of money, and since one of the biggest disturbances is the squabbling of children over toys, it is imperative that the parents either buy nothing, or else they must buy each child, depending on age and regardless of sex, the identical toy in every respect, even down to the slightest detail, otherwise this difference may arouse desire which cannot be satisfied. Let me clarify this.

If you placed on the dinner table a pitcher of lemonade and a pitcher of milk, one child may prefer the former while the second selects the latter, but both were given an equal opportunity to satisfy their desire for either one, which does not in any way blame their desire. Could you possibly put on the table enough milk for one child and enough lemonade for two? Wouldn't this obviously blame the desire of one child should both children desire the milk? "Mommy, Johnny got a glass of milk and I want some too." Isn't this just plain common sense, which you refer to as fairness? Children observe the slightest shade of discrimination in dividing things, as you well know, and will resent you for taking something away from them which is what you do when you are not equitable.

If you give a little boy a toy soldier and a girl a doll what is this but an encouragement for them to quarrel? Why shouldn't the boy want to play with the doll and the girl with the soldier, and should both desire the doll at the same time, what then? Let's watch Daddy solve the problem.

"Jimmy, this doll belongs to Diane" (this teaches possessiveness and unconsciously justifies while encouraging Jimmy's desire to take her doll, if not now, later); "dolls are for little girls not for boys," which is wholly fallacious but existed out of necessity in the world of free will.

"But I wanna play widda dolly."

"Diane, you be a big girl" (this blames him for not being big about it) "and let Jimmy play with the doll just for a little while and you play with his soldier."

"Dolly mine, you buy for Diane, and dolls for goils, Daddy, you just told Jimmy; Jimmy not a goil."

All this can be prevented by realizing that every child must be given an equal opportunity to be happy, which is denied when parents set up fallacious standards of what is for a girl and what is for a boy. If you give two girls, one blue the other a red doll, this encourages them to desire what the other has, and arguments are bound to result; but if they wake up to discover that each has the identical toy there can be no possessiveness, no jealousy, no envy, and what is much more important, no fighting to disturb your evening. Neither has to be told that both have the same toy; they see this for themselves, and it makes no difference which one is picked up because they are identical. Isn't this just plain common sense?

However, just as soon as children are taught what it means that man's will is not free, that's how soon you can desist from concerning yourself about the various things mentioned. For example, if two boys have one bike and know what it means that will is not free, neither could selfishly desire this bike without considering the other, because they know this would never be blamed, which compels them to discover an equitable manner to distribute the time. If the hours it can be used are six either child will select at random from a hat the first or second three hours, and the one who uses the bike first will never have to be reminded when his time is up because the knowledge that he could stay out for the entire six hours without being blamed by anyone, though he knows it would hurt his brother who would not want to hurt him in return, compels him to be very dissatisfied at the thought of being even one minute late. These are mathematical relations that all mankind can see when extended properly.

But clothes are not toys and present a different kind of problem. What is put on a child is his, just as his arm and leg, his toothbrush and bed, are his. Boys and girls know, quickly enough, they are different from one another, and one would never desire or envy the clothes of the other. However, one little girl may envy what her sister has by the way mommy makes over her clothes, which prevents all mothers from showing any outward sign that they are pleased with the way a child is dressed. You could dress children in entirely different clothes, and it would make not one whit of difference to them because what they wear is not a source of fun... until they are taught to see that certain type clothes, certain color combinations, certain shaped faces, certain figures, certain color eyes, hair, etc., receive praise and compliments. If you should say, "Oh, what a lovely dress," her sister, who may not have gotten the same compliment, will place a value on this type and color dress, this type of individual, etc., and be envious of her sister for having something she doesn't have, and this is a real hurt; but without the compliment there can be no envy. This holds true with all words that praise or compliment another, like cute, pretty, darling, beautiful, handsome, etc., which teaches children to place a value on something about themselves or others which arouses these expressions, and when other children see that these compliments are not directed to them they become jealous of their sisters, brothers, and others while unconsciously resenting their parents for this discrimination. However, when this blanket of blame is removed, it will be impossible to say a dress is cute because no one will ever judge or criticize its appearance. The way you dress yourself and your children at the present time depends on what others think, for you didn't like having your husband, your children or yourself being ridiculed, but when you know well in advance that no one will ever again blame you or judge how you should dress, speak, walk, etc., what difference does it make to you what color dress your child wears just so she likes it. But as to what a girl will wear when she is on the make for a husband will definitely arouse desire. Our males can't stand going to the beaches unless they are prepared for marriage because they are constantly getting invitations. Consequently, the boys get married very young, between 16 and 18. Did I hear one of your psychologists say this was too young? He is so in the habit of judging what is right for others that he can't get out of it that easily, but if he wants to know if this age is really too young, let him take a trip to our planet and ask the boys and girls who have to make the decision for themselves.

You are prevented from criticizing or ridiculing the way I dress because you know that this ridicule is a definite source of hurt, and your knowledge that I will never blame you for hurting me this way because I must consider your desire as beyond your control, makes it impossible for you to derive any satisfaction from being excused for what you cannot justify and you know you can prevent if you want to. It's the same old story over and over again.

Henceforth, there will be only one standard for children and parents, the happiness of each, but in an unconscious manner, the happiness of parents up until now was the unhappiness of their children. Durant was happy when he got his daughter to go to bed and was not moved even when she pleaded with her dimpled arms around his neck, but she was unhappy at that moment. She was happy when she didn't practice the piano, but he was unhappy at this, which made him impose his will on her for his happiness, not hers. He was happy to see her drink plenty of milk and eat loads of whole wheat bread, but had she been left alone and given the opportunity to choose among other foods, she no doubt would have been much happier because her taste plays an important role. This relation between parents and children is so interwoven with resentment that in many cases the latter will refuse to eat what they might enjoy because the former tells them they will, which blames the possibility that they won't. "Here is something real nice mommy just prepared; you will like it." "I don't want it and I won't like it." "How do you know when you haven't even tasted it yet?"

The child takes this opportunity to get unconscious satisfaction out of hurting mother because she has hurt him so many times by standing in the way of his desires, and just the knowledge that she wants him to eat it because it is good is sufficient proof to his mind that it is bad. Durant, however, was able to control his daughter simply because he reduced the amount of her unhappiness to a minimum in comparison to the average home; and by hiding his authority behind psychological tricks which he thought was wisdom, he was able to get her to love her daddy very much. But in other homes his psychology was not applied, and the parents didn't hesitate to punish children severely, which developed terrible guilt complexes because they were taught to honor their mother and father. Durant employed the exact same psychology with his daughter as an expert male uses when winning the love of a girl, but neither shows their own love. There is no question but how much Ethel loved her father as a little girl, but this love would have been much greater had he not been compelled by God's will to set up these fallacious standards of value. By discovering that man's will is not free and what this means, you are compelled to remove the standards which allow the greatest happiness imaginable to exist in all homes, in a manner far superior to what anybody on your planet now experiences.

Once a mother realizes that she can no longer blame her children for anything, regardless of what they do, she is compelled to prevent those very things for which blame and punishment were previously necessary. However, in most cases, she blames and yells at them not because they were hurting her or themselves in any way, but because she resents their disobedience. It will soon be discovered that this blame of the parents is a safety valve that permitted them to shift their responsibility. Consequently, when mom sees that she can no longer rush the children in the morning, that she can no longer blame them for not having their clothes ready, she is compelled to prepare everything well in advance or teach them, without blame, how to take care of themselves. Every bit of the hurt that exists between parents and children is occasioned by the former constantly trying to impose their will, nothing else.

Where eating is concerned, this is the mother's responsibility. Since she is not running a restaurant and cannot blame the children for not eating what she cooks, she is given no choice but to prepare everything in such a tasty manner that her entire family looks forward to eating every meal. Since it is impossible for her to judge that certain foods have greater value than others where another body is concerned, unless science has established mathematical facts, she will be compelled to arrange a diversified variety over an entire week or two weeks so that her children and husband will look forward to eating certain meals on certain days. If the family, for example, likes spaghetti and meatballs which is served on Monday, that morning they will look forward to the evening when they will be served what they like. Tuesday morning, knowing that mother will have something else that evening, they again anticipate the evening, just as they may look forward to a certain television show or something else. This is a great happiness, looking forward to what gives pleasure, and eating is something we do all our lives. By setting up each day for a specific meal no one can ever get tired of eating the same thing, and when the week rolls around, everybody is looking forward to spaghetti again. Today, however, mother serves so many meals the kids do not like that they are compelled to fill up on cookies, candy, ice cream, etc., and when Thanksgiving approaches, the family looks forward to turkey as if this is the only time of the year one can have a Thanksgiving dinner.

The very fact that pie, cake, ice cream, etc., are called dessert places a greater value on these items, which makes children look forward to this dessert with every meal, and yet I can understand the concern of parents when their children eat too much candy, etc. However, this habit can easily be broken without blaming the child and without removing these pleasures from the life of a family. All that is necessary is to include these items not as a dessert, but as part of the meal itself on certain days. Do you eat steak for every meal, chicken, spinach? Why then should you have dessert, milk, bread with every meal? These are habits which reveal that man has not been doing much thinking on your planet, just following. A mother could very easily arrange a schedule so that all these items of dessert could be included. Ice cream could be served during one meal, not as dessert but as something else to be eaten that is enjoyed, and when the meal is over the children will look forward to the next meal without expecting ice cream because this is served on another day, just as steak or chicken, bread and spinach. When this day rolls around, they will look forward to the entire meal, which includes the ice cream, cake or candy. Just bear in mind there is only so much an individual can eat, and if he is left alone and is not blamed with your fallacious values, he can only go in one direction. Under these conditions, a child would no more think of eating ice cream and candy between meals than of eating vegetables and meat. But to accomplish this mother is compelled to prepare a variety of tasty dinners because she can blame nobody anymore if they don't eat.

Another fallacy that is completely exploded is the belief that certain foods and beverages are for adults only. "No, dear, you can't have coffee, this is for grownups." Have you any conception of how many people eat and drink what they have acquired a taste for, not because they liked it from the start, but because they were determined to do what others, whom they admire, are doing? The very fact that children are told point-blank that coffee, cigarettes, and liquor are not for them until they become adults places a fallacious value on becoming an adult, and gives to these items a strong appeal. Some boys have gotten sick smoking cigars because they were determined to oppose the wishes of their parents, and girls have become promiscuous because they were constantly judged and blamed before anything was even done. Don't do this and you can't have that are challenges to children who resent authority.

Consequently, there is nothing *wrong* with children smoking cigarettes, cigars, chewing tobacco, drinking coffee, beer, liquor, highballs, eating loads and loads of candy, cake, ice cream, and anything else, provided they want to. However, their wanting to eat the latter in excess, as was pointed out, is within your power to control without any form of blame, while the other can be completely wiped out from the desires of your children also without any form of blame, that is, unless you want your children to smoke cigars, drink beer, etc.

In the new world, the children will never hear that certain things are for adults and other things for children.

A young child at the dinner table will be given his choice of beverages. There is no reason for Dad to drink his beer or highball, coffee, and tea surreptitiously. Every person at the table will be given an equal opportunity to have what the others have, without any psychological influences. Do you think it is possible, when all these influences are removed, for a child to prefer coffee, beer, tea, liquor, wine to milk? Children do not have to ask permission to try this or that. If you are worried that your little girl may become a drunkard or smoke cigars, then you had better remove everything that you like from the table which makes you happy, because there is no way you can prevent this imaginative possibility without blame in some form. Durant prevented his daughter from staying downstairs, but he was compelled to blame her desire. The only alternative was to go to sleep early himself, which certainly could not make him happy, so is he given a choice when blame is removed? If you have to give up everything you like for the happiness of your children, you will soon be miserable, but you don't have to give up anything once the truth is understood. The very moment all fallacious values are removed, which are frozen into the habitual use of words and expression, children will eat, drink, and do only what they really want to do of their own free will. You couldn't make children do by force what they do not like, but yet in your present world, they are compelled to do what they really do not enjoy only because of some fallacious value that is imposed in a negative or positive manner. As a consequence of obeying God's will, Thou Shall Not Blame in any form, within two generations, the desire for alcoholic beverages and smoking will be reduced to an absolute minimum, because when all psychological influences are removed, it is impossible to desire what you really do not like. Obviously, advertising plays a great role in creating a desire for these things, and remember, we cannot tell these people what to do, so just be patient and see what happens in the next two chapters.

But what will parents teach their children about cleanliness, keeping their room tidy, their beds made, clothes hung up, and what about *good manners*, how to speak to others, how to hold one's knife and fork, how to act in society?

It is obvious that up until a child is able to do certain things for himself, the mother will have to do them. She will wash, dress, and feed him, keeping his room clean. She will desire to do these things not only because she knows her husband would never blame her if she did not, but also because not doing them only reveals to her husband that she is not in love with him, and this is impossible to desire when her sexual security and happiness depend on showing her love. However, the mother will teach the child not only by setting examples but by asking the child if he wants to learn how to do specific things, like tie his shoes and dress himself. He will have a natural desire to learn, but under no circumstances must mother ever blame the slowness of his learning nor compliment his success. She will ask him if he would like to learn how to make his own bed, hang up his own clothes, and do all the things that she has been doing for him. Little by little, without any persuasion or blame, the child will develop a habit of making his bed every morning, putting his things away, etc. If on some mornings when the habit has not yet taken hold, mother will not blame him in any way but will continue helping him to develop in the direction he wants to go. No child will consider it a distasteful duty as long as mother doesn't communicate this idea, and mother will be prevented, in the new world, from ever thinking of it as such. Consequently, it will just be a matter of time before the habit will be successfully developed, and the children will get great satisfaction in taking care of their own room just as a little baby learning to walk, or learning to eat with a spoon, takes great satisfaction in succeeding without assistance; but remember, no applause, no compliments, no praise, no nickels and dimes. The pleasure in keeping his room in order will come from the pleasure of keeping his room in order, and from nothing else. The pleasure he will experience in washing and brushing his teeth will come from the pleasure of feeling clean.

At the dinner table, he will be shown how to use a knife, fork, and spoon, not because this is good manners, but because he may find greater pleasure in eating with them. If, however, he should drop his fork and use his hands, he cannot be blamed; even if he should lay the utensil down and prefer his hands, he cannot be corrected in any way, as this blames him for doing something wrong, and he is not doing anything wrong. Furthermore, if he should pick up the fork that was dropped without wiping it off, this again cannot be corrected or criticized unless you can do this without blame in any form. This reveals that what harm a family perceived in this wiping away of germs existed only as a figment of their imagination. Furthermore, if a child comes into dinner after play and does not wash his hands, he cannot be corrected or criticized, for he is not hurting anybody, and for you to say, "Go wash your hands, Jimmy, this instant," blames him for not washing them. However, these habits of washing before dinner can easily be developed without blame. Good manners are the respect of the other person and his desires, but in your present world, the very people who have been trying to teach what they call good manners only reveal that they are disrespectful, insincere, selfish, and that they have the worst manners of anybody. Let me clarify this.

If I were at your home for dinner and did not take off my hat at the dinner table, you would say I have no manners, and if I picked up the steak with my hands, you would be positively convinced that I lived where there was no civilization. But in reality, if this annoys you, it only shows that you have no manners not your guest, because how I consume my food is my business, which makes no imposition on your desire to eat any way you desire, but your desire that I eat with a knife and fork while removing my hat indicates that the sacrifice of my desire is what you require to be happy, and this pure and simple is selfishness, bad manners and disrespect. Frankly, I wouldn't care if you breaded the steak on the floor for yourself and covered it with ants, for this is your business, not mine, and if it makes you happy, more power to you. The fact that you have been brought up a certain way makes you judge others in the light of your standards, and when they fall short you have something to criticize which to you reveals your superiority; but now that God is removing all these fallacious standards the person who before felt self-conscious in your presence is made to feel at home wherever he goes throughout Earth.

However, he knows that keeping his hat on does not hurt you in any way, but if he came to dinner wearing dirty clothes that gave off an odor he knows that this might be annoying, and the realization that you would never even blame him for this annoyance which is real, not a figment of the imagination, makes him desire to come to dinner without any offensive odors the result, generally, of uncleanliness; and if he sat down in a movie with his hat on the person behind might not get a clear view, and knowing this annoyance would never be blamed, that he would never get tapped on the shoulder with, "Hey pal, I can't see, your hat is in the way," compels him to desire removing it because the thought that he would never get blamed for this real annoyance, which he knows is his responsibility, is a motion in the direction of dissatisfaction. However, if he was unaware of someone behind him, a gentle reminder from this person would be greatly appreciated, not resented. Good manners can be defined very simply, it is minding one's own business, and minding one's own business is very simply never blaming another for anything he desires to do, regardless of what this might be. But as was shown the knowledge that he will not be blamed for hurting another only compels him to desire preventing the hurt which before was blamed and punished. However, this can only apply when both parties involved in an action know what it means that man's will is not free. This is God's mathematical manner in revealing for the first time what is a real and what is an imaginary hurt. The offense of my odor at your dinner table is real, but my wearing a hat or eating with my hands is an imaginary offense that cannot exist once these fallacious standards are removed.

Remember, if anything annoys you, regardless of what it is, you have a perfect right to try your utmost to correct it, but this must be done without blaming another person because man's will is not free; and if this confuses you I suggest that you read this book over from the very beginning.

If you don't like your children coming to the dinner table without washing their hands you are perfectly at liberty to correct this in any manner you see fit, just so you don't blame the children in any way, shape, or form. However, if you cannot solve this problem don't let it worry you because no one is going to criticize you for this, and nothing is going to happen to the children other than becoming happier and happier at not being bossed around for this essentially is the whole problem. The very things you don't like, other people telling you how to live your life, is the very thing you impose on your offspring.

Your telling children what is right and wrong is the consequence of fallacious fears as well as real fears that will vanish with this blanket of blame. It is understandable that you should want your child to graduate from high school because, in your present environment, this is judged valuable. Consequently, the parents push their children in the direction of this value, even if force is necessary. Durant was no different than these other fathers where the end result was concerned; he, however, exercised a psychological technique which made his daughter desire this value so that force would not have to be used, as he did with the piano.

Because of this stratification of values, hundreds of businesses have come into existence for the purpose of helping others get more out of life. What is teaching a child how to speak, walk, act, but teaching how to consider oneself superior to another? If one child says yes and another says yeah, there are those who actually believe that the tone of this one-syllable word reveals some form of superiority. However, you are going to be quite surprised as all these fallacious standards of value are compelled to take leave of your planet by mathematical necessity.

There are certain problems that confront parents that cannot be handled in the usual manner this book has outlined, which requires a deeper analysis and permits me to recall an anecdote that will adequately introduce the problem while revealing the great confusion of psychologists.

One in particular, who visited my home with his little boy for the express purpose of telling me about a new principle being applied (nothing should be done to inhibit the desires of a child, but especially — no punishment) suddenly discovered himself in a position to demonstrate his opinion when his little boy, getting restless, decided to use my brand new sofa for a trampoline. The father was somewhat embarrassed and tried his utmost to get the boy off without using force. "Jimmy, now you know this isn't the right thing to do, so please come off there right away." But Jimmy was having too much fun, and he appeared to be getting just as much satisfaction out of his father not being able to do anything about it, for he knew that dad wouldn't hit or punish him for anything. Finally, Dad just reached up and took the boy off, but even then, Jimmy jumped right back on. He at last told the boy that if he didn't go back on, he would stop at a trampoline place and let him jump to his heart's content, and if one wasn't open, he would give him something else to make up for it. Now the question arises, how is it humanly possible to get the boy off without blaming his desire?

Actually, the psychologist was right about not inhibiting the desire of a child in any way, provided this was applied while knowing that man's will is not free and what this means; otherwise, a tremendous amount of harm could be done to children as well as parents. The same condition would prevail, to draw up a comparison, if suddenly all laws, government, and forms of legal punishment were withdrawn without knowing that man's will is not free; can you imagine what would happen? Every potential thief, and even those who never thought about stealing would have a ball, and nobody would be safe. Can you imagine what Russia, China, Cuba, even the United States would do if there were no other powers to control the desire to spread whatever each country desired to spread? This very fact, that the moment man understands what it means that will is not free prevents the very things for which government came into existence, proves, beyond a shadow of doubt, the reality of God, this amazing mathematical power. Everything was timed so perfectly that you must catch your breath in absolute amazement when you contemplate the magnificence of this mathematical equation, which includes not only the solar system and everything that exists on each planet in relation, but it includes man himself and all the evil and ignorance that ever existed.

Consequently, by applying the psychology just mentioned at the wrong time, these children were compelled to become little spoiled monsters who took advantage of their parents at every turn, and this was the kind of situation that existed between Jimmy and his father. I met one doctor whose child was so spoiled rotten that it was miserable living with the child, but the poor father, having no way of knowing what was right and wrong except to follow what he was taught by the experts, was given no choice since he was made to believe that punishing a child was still worse.

Now the solution to this problem is very simple. The moment all parents understand what it means that man's will is not free, they are to distinguish very carefully between what is and what is not a real hurt. If the children can be made to understand that even though they should hurt someone in a real manner they will still not be blamed, which means that they can be taught the principles in this book, then of course nothing further has to be done with them; but if they are too young to understand, then you must tell them that if they continue hurting others in a concrete manner they will be punished in a specific manner, which leaves it up to their choice. If Jimmy had known that jumping on someone's sofa is a form of hurt for which his father would definitely punish him, then before jumping on my sofa, he would have thought twice. However, this cannot be used unless what the child does is a definite form of hurt to someone, not an imaginary hurt, such as used by Durant. Within a very short while, no child will desire to hurt another, not so much because he knows he will be punished for this hurt, but primarily because his parents have stopped hurting him by constantly standing in the way of his desire. But remember, there are two desires involved — yours and your child's — and it is not a form of blame in any way should you decide not to satisfy the desire of your child when your own desire is involved — unless you gave your child reason to believe that you would satisfy this desire.

Once your children are taught what it means that man's will is not free, they will not desire to ask you for anything; but you, knowing this, will ask them if there is anything you can do, while they, knowing that you will never blame their suggestion, will be prevented from taking advantage of your generosity. My daughter knows that I would never ask her to get me a glass of water, no matter how thirsty I might be; but seeing me perspire she, of her own free will or desire, will say, "Dad, can I get you a glass of ice water?" and I know she cannot have any other motive than to make me happy in this instance for to use this to impose an obligation would only tacitly blame me and justify my not doing what otherwise I would. Knowing that she cannot drive a car and that she would never ask me for any kind of favor compels me to ask her if I might drive her anywhere or ask if there is anything I might do to make her happy, and she, knowing that I would never blame her suggestion, regardless of what it was, is compelled not to take advantage of my generosity. Are you beginning to recognize the difference between living in one world and the other?

If your child does not know that man's will is not free and should ask you to run her somewhere with the car, you are perfectly at liberty to say no simply because your desire is involved, and if she nags you to take her it is within your right to tell her that she is now hurting you with her complaint, for which she will be punished if it continues. But even this can be avoided by setting up some sort of reasonable schedule until children can be taught the principles in this book. This is the heart of the problem — teaching everyone what it means that man's will is not free, and by the end of this book, you will be on pins and needles to start your Great Transition. Remember, if there is anything you don't understand, just take your time and read it over and over again. This entire book is completely mathematical in every way, and once you learn how to perceive these relations, it will be just as easy to understand as two plus two equals four, which also cannot be denied.

In concluding this chapter, let me remind you that from the time children are born, you cannot blame them for anything they desire to do, which means that you are compelled to prevent, without any form of tacit blame, what you do not want. To arouse their desire for an end you have determined is best, such as classical music over jazz or piano over saxophone, is a definite form of tacit blame, but to tell them that they can learn any instrument they wish after hearing them all or can buy the type of music they want after listening to the differences in sound, is quite a different thing. One method does not consider the desire of the children, which is the source of all contention because you feel you know what is better, right, good, etc., while the other method does, which reveals true parental love. However, to ease your fears about what is right and wrong just remember this simple rule: If you are unable to prevent your children from desiring what you feel will be a hurt, or from not desiring what you think will be for their benefit (both without any form of blame), then it is rather obvious that what you like or dislike for them and cannot prevent without blame is something not in any way harmful, existing only as an imaginary fear based upon false knowledge, otherwise you would definitely have the power to prevent this harm without blame in any form. But should the hurt be to you or another, which came into existence as a consequence of various relations that developed over the years (and be a real, not imaginary hurt), then it is necessary to give the child a choice between hurting others and being punished, which will not be necessary when children are taught these principles or brought up by parents who themselves have been taught.

PART THREE

The extension of a mathematical relation into the world of business, government, and the accumulation of knowledge

CHAPTER 6 — The End of All War and Crime

CHAPTER 7 — The New World

CHAPTER 8 — Education

CHAPTER 6 — The End of All War and Crime

And now, my friends, you are about to behold an actual miracle, as the knowledge that man's will is not free and what this means not only puts a mathematical end to the possibility of war and crime, but completely changes the entire economic system of Earth from one of competition to one of complete cooperation. I know this sounds fantastic, but it is true, nevertheless. Any scientist who has made an undeniable discovery doesn't need your approval for its validity, though he does require your understanding for recognition. If the answer to this mathematical problem is five (if it takes three cows two weeks to eat two acres of grass plus all that grows on the two acres in two weeks, and if it takes two cows four weeks to eat two acres of grass plus all that grows on the two acres in the four weeks, how many cows would be required to eat six acres in six weeks plus all that grows on the six acres in the six weeks?), do I need you to tell me if it is right or wrong? Gregor Mendel received posthumous recognition because those to whom he first submitted his discovery considered themselves the judges of whether it was true or false, not realizing that the mathematical relations revealing its truth were beyond their perception. There is quite a difference between discrediting

163

what a person writes because it is judged false as a consequence of it appearing fantastic, and admitting the possibility that it still may be true. I take the time at this point to mention the difference because if you were to judge the changes about to take place in terms of your present knowledge and understanding your unconscious ignorance would be compelled to deny even the possibility, therefore it is of the utmost importance for you to realize that the validity of the knowledge about to be imparted doesn't depend on your approval, although your ability to understand these mathematical or undeniable relations is necessary for recognition.

Is it humanly possible for you to believe that the solution to the problem of war and crime involves the end of all government, or, to phrase it more appropriately, since many aspects of government will continue to function, the end of all authority and control? Is it possible for you to believe that millions upon millions of people will be permanently displaced from their jobs, professions, and businesses without being hurt in any way? Is it possible for you to believe that your murderers and other criminals will soon be released from prison and accorded the same consideration and respect as the President of the United States?

Because this is a very crucial point in my book it is imperative that you completely understand what is meant by the mathematical corollary Thou Shall Not Blame, so I suggest that you reread the second chapter in order to fully comprehend why any person who judges what is right for another is absolutely wrong (as two plus two equals five is wrong) since it strikes the first blow and demonstrates how any judgment of another before something is done is an advance accusation which offers unconscious justification to do what is criticized by the standard imposed in the tacit blame. In other words, if you know that you can prevent the very thing you do not want by being a certain way — are you given a choice? Consequently, the very first thing this book reveals in a mathematical manner is that no individual or group of individuals can ever again desire to govern another because it will be seen that not governing is truly better for themselves. Can the President of the United States possibly desire to tell others what to do when it can be revealed in a mathematical manner that such authority will only result in the very war he is making efforts to prevent? If every member of the government who is engaged in telling others what is right and wrong should learn that the most harmonious relations imaginable will exist on Earth the moment all government comes to an end, are these people given a choice if this is really what they want? Can't you see the great humor?

When a politician runs for office, he is primarily interested in getting elected, having an income from this source, and being in the limelight — not in the welfare of the people. This is easily proven by the fact that it is never a source of satisfaction to be denied what gives you satisfaction. Can the President and Prime Minister find satisfaction in being denied the privilege of making speeches as to what they are going to accomplish, even though this denial results in the very things they have been purporting to do? How is it humanly possible for a salesman who depends on sales for a livelihood to be happy to learn that what he is selling will no longer be required because everybody now has it? Can it be a source of satisfaction to lose his income, which he desperately needs? It is impossible for government to discover the solution when this entails the removal of government, just as it is impossible for your doctors and psychiatrists to discover the cure for all sickness when this necessitates the removal of all psychiatry and 90 percent of the medical profession; but when these people learn that they are going to be guaranteed their present income for the rest of their lives for doing absolutely nothing they will suddenly realize how uncertain they have always been of how much of their ignorance passed for knowledge and how much of their knowledge was nothing but an unconscious effort to conceal their ignorance from themselves and others. This does not mean that the doctors and politicians, theologians and philosophers are responsible for what now exists, but their removal is necessary for the cure which will come about of their own free will.

Now there are many people in the world who make a profit from war, for which they cannot be blamed, and there are many theologians and politicians who cannot derive any satisfaction from having their playthings, so to speak, taken away. Consequently this group will be somewhat blinded to the mathematical relations, and will be compelled to search for some flaw in order to retain their accustomed position of extreme spiritual satisfaction, which necessitates that you, who do not want war and crime (as with a boy and girl who do not desire being hurt), to learn the mathematical secret of how to prevent what you do not want. However, there isn't any flaw which compels every person who is accustomed to giving orders, as is the case with religion, government, and education, to be absolutely silent for the very first time while the truth about man's nature is being revealed. In other words, your education cannot be used as a standard to determine the validity of the knowledge in this book, regardless of who or what you are, since every relation in this book is absolutely undeniable to those who have the capacity to perceive them. Consequently, this book is an SOS to the thinking group of the human race; otherwise, your ignorance will laugh at and criticize what you cannot understand. Nevertheless —

As was demonstrated in the second and verified in the following chapters, when man judges in advance what is right for someone else, which tacitly blames the desire to do what is considered wrong, he actually offers unconscious justification to do the very things not desired by himself. Consequently, you are given no choice regarding the first step that must be taken in the prevention of war.

Since a girl can only offer her body without fear of being hurt when the boy knows that she will never hold him responsible in any way, or blame him for having a good time and leaving, it is obvious that the first step is for this knowledge that man's will is not free to be translated into every language and disseminated throughout your planet so that the United States or any nation who wishes to disarm can do so without any fear of being attacked. Then, when this is accomplished, every bit of tacit blame will be removed from all human relations without any fear of being hurt. In other words, the United States is unaware that if Russia strikes, it is the second blow only because this was unconsciously justified by the former striking the first blow, or vice versa. Therefore the knowledge revealed in this book plainly instructs the people on your planet, once it is translated into all languages, that any nation who is armed is actually striking the first blow once it is understood that man's will is not free, which indicates that any nation who disarms does not wish to harm another human being regardless of what is done to hurt its own people, simply because this knowledge makes it mathematically clear that it is absolutely impossible to be attacked when the attacker knows well in advance that this nation will be compelled to excuse what must be considered as beyond control. Consequently, by disarming completely this nation says in effect: "If you wish to attack us, hurt us, rob us, murder us, please go right ahead without the slightest fear of retaliation because we know that you are only obeying God's will over which you have no control, which compels us to excuse your actions no matter how much you hurt us." But you know you are not compelled to hurt these people unless you want to, and when it fully dawns on you that no matter how much you hurt this nation, you will never be blamed, criticized or hurt in return, it becomes mathematically impossible to derive any satisfaction from the contemplation of this terrible crime when the conditions prevent any possibility of justification. This means that the very moment the United States makes it universally known that she is desisting immediately from all forms of judging what is right for another, which includes the arms that tacitly blame the possibility of an attack, every nation is compelled of their own free will to refrain from hurting the United States because no one can get satisfaction from being excused for that of which the responsibility could never be denied or justified. Consequently, the second step to the end of all war is to immediately disarm after the knowledge that man's will is not free is disseminated throughout your planet.

At the present time it is impossible to disarm because each nation fears a treacherous attack, but when it is known that under no conditions will any retaliatory measures be taken because it is impossible to desire hurting someone for doing what he is compelled to do, no nation can desire to attack for this could never be a source of satisfaction. By turning the other cheek, Gandhi and his people demonstrated how they were able to prevent the second cheek from being struck, although many lives were lost. By revealing the knowledge that man's will is not free and what this actually means, each individual makes known in advance that he is turning his cheek no matter what is done to him because he cannot find satisfaction in blaming another for doing what he is compelled to do even if it means a terrible hurt to himself; and this mathematically prevents his first cheek from being struck because there is no way satisfaction can be gotten under these conditions. However, if the United States was tacitly blaming Russia through some economic means, then disarming would be as effective as the announcement of a tyrant that he is not going to judge what is right for his people while starving them. Consequently, there are other factors to be considered, but the first two steps are absolutely required as a prerequisite to ending all war. That's right, my friends! The solution to the immediate end of all war is that simple because nothing is causing you to go to war — unless you want to — and there is nothing that can make you want to once the tacit blame of armaments is removed, for this advance accusation, this fear of being attacked, unconsciously justifies and excuses the very things not desired; but in the world of free will you were justified because your unconscious ignorance created an atmosphere in which being different than you were would only have made matters worse, therefore you had no choice.

Now, once this knowledge is disseminated throughout your planet, every single weapon that is designed to hurt another individual or prevent the satisfaction of his desire, regardless of what it is, will be immediately destroyed without the slightest fear of being harmed as a consequence. But remember, these weapons are destroyed not because they are forms of tacit blame, but only because with the aid of this slide rule, you are able to see for the first time what is truly better for yourself.

Furthermore, every possibility of committing a crime will vanish the very moment everything that stands in the way of such an act is removed. Consequently, the military and police forces will retire while their weapons are destroyed, all prisons will be demolished, and every prisoner released after being taught the principles in this book, and no one need have the slightest fear that a crime will be committed, especially when all the other forms of tacit blame are also removed. All locks, vaults, armored cars, burglar alarms, etc., will become obsolete at the very time they are destroyed, and everything that tries in some way to prevent the desire of another from being satisfied, which tries in some way to prevent stealing what belongs to another, will be removed simply because this will mathematically prevent the desire to hurt someone as a consequence of this tacit blame. Montaigne perceived part of this relation as did Edward Gibbon, but they were too confused with words to disentangle the cobwebs. Now observe tacit blame in the business world.

It is obvious that an employer is anxious to get the best possible men for any jobs that are available; this is the reason he screens his applicants. However, this screening is a definite form of tacit blame which justifies any efforts to lie in order to get the position; but when an applicant knows that he is not going to be questioned as to his qualifications, when he knows that he will never be blamed regardless of how many mistakes he makes, that he will never be criticized or punished by being fired, he is given no choice but to forgo any job for which there is the least possible doubt in his mind that he may not be able to handle. Consequently, by removing this tacit blame, every individual who seeks employment is compelled to prefer developing a skill so that he can apply for a job with the confidence that he will never hurt someone, for which he would never be blamed.

A creditor, by pressing his debtors, gives them unconscious justification to shirk this responsibility. But once the debtors know that man's will is not free, which makes them realize that their creditor will never ask them again for what they owe him since they know he will consider their not paying him back a compulsion over which they have no control even though they know it is not beyond their control, they will be compelled of their own free will to desire paying back every penny since it gives them no satisfaction to be excused for hurting him when every bit of justification for this hurt has been removed.

In borrowing money or buying on credit, the seller or lender in your present world is compelled to keep a record in order not to be cheated out of his money, but in your new world about to unfold the buyer or borrower is compelled to keep the records because he knows that no one will ever blame him if he never pays back a single dime. In your present circumstances you are always compelled to ask for credit and loans which are refused, but under the new conditions it is impossible to tacitly blame the seller by asking for credit simply because you know that he is there to move merchandise, and the very moment you know you are able to buy what he has, a sale is consummated without any forms or contracts to be signed since the seller knows, just as certain as two plus two equals four, that it will be mathematically impossible for you to buy what he has without paying for it when you know that he will never blame you in any way should you not. Consequently, all sales slips, contracts, credit applications, collection agencies, and investigators of all sorts are displaced, along with lawyers, accountants, personnel departments, etc. Furthermore, all cashiers and cash registers are displaced because they obviously blame the honesty of others, while even money itself is displaced because it tacitly blames the desire of an individual to spend more than he has; and since it is impossible to sell an identical item at a different price without blame, it is obvious that all forms of economic competition must come to an end. This obviously puts an end to all forms of advertising, the mint, banks as a place to safeguard money, and all checking accounts, for this is the same as money. There are many others who are displaced as a consequence of this tremendous transition, but it shouldn't be necessary to list every one since you can do this for yourself. I know this sounds fantastic but don't jump to any conclusions; and remember, the inception of your Golden Age does not begin because everybody stops judging but only because by understanding what it means that man's will is not free you are allowed to foresee what is truly better for yourself which engenders the desire to give up this tacit blame of others and automatically destroys further need for economic competition and government. Communism and capitalism willingly give up their present system because both see an opportunity to become happier, wealthier, and healthier as a consequence, without the slightest possibility of war and the utmost in freedom. Under the reign of free will, this transition to a cooperative Earth was a mathematical impossibility because no one knew what was truly better for himself, although many thought they knew. Consequently, force was an absolute requirement to prevent further harm, but not anymore, since this knowledge prevents the very acts of evil for which blame and punishment were previously necessary.

The solution to this problem requires that every person on your planet be satisfied; otherwise, it is obvious that God is showing partiality, and how this is accomplished reveals the most infinite wisdom imaginable. I shall now demonstrate this in the next chapter.

CHAPTER 7 — The New World

It should be apparent to your perception that once you understand what it means that man's will is not free, money as a medium of exchange becomes a useless appendage, for no one will ever again tell you what to do in the form of laws and authority. Consequently, all that is necessary is to transfer your personal business into a record book, which each individual will keep for that purpose. If your income is $100 per week, and you just spent $75, you would simply show a savings of $25.00. The fact that money will be dispensed with does not decrease the purchasing power of your millionaires, nor does it increase that of the poor; and the only purpose of dispensing with it is simply because it entails a tremendous amount of wasted labor, which tacitly blames the honesty of man. However, under the new conditions it is mathematically impossible to be dishonest, not only because you know you will never be blamed no matter how much you hurt another by stealing his property, but also because every person alive will recognize in the great transition about to take place an undeniable benefit for himself. Remember, you are perfectly free to cheat, steal, rob, kill, do anything you want to do with any fear of being blamed or punished because it is now known that man is compelled to do everything he does, but how is it humanly possible to desire cheating when you know that no one will ever ask you for an accounting of your little record book, when *you* will know whether you are cheating which knowledge that you will never be blamed no matter what you do mathematically prevents any possibility of justification absolutely necessary for satisfaction? Under these conditions, I repeat, it is mathematically impossible for any person to desire taking advantage of not being blamed because it is definitely not to his advantage.

However, it is extremely important for every individual to know that what came about on your planet was exactly as it was supposed to be. This, of course, doesn't mean that the future will continue like the past, but it does mean that no one is to blame in any way for what happened and consequently everyone is permitted to turn himself upside down for the purpose of dumping out anything and everything for which he holds himself responsible; but remember you are prevented from repeating an action that formerly hurt someone by the knowledge that you will never be blamed for what you know you can prevent, giving you no satisfaction. You are completely absolved of all responsibility for anything you have ever done in the past and will never be blamed by anyone in the future, but the present is your very own responsibility since no one will ever again tell you what to do or what is better for yourself. Furthermore, the knowledge that man's will is not free mathematically reveals that no person is any better than another, regardless of how much he has in his head or how much in his pocket, and regardless of his color, creed, education, etc. The present stratified position of wealth cannot be blamed, but within two or three generations (don't worry about death, which will be clarified in the last chapter), the difference that may still exist will be absolutely negligible simply because every income will be identical, which brings up a very important question.

Would it disturb you, think very carefully before answering, if the janitor also had steak for dinner, just as long as this does not encroach on your own purchasing power? Does your satisfaction lie in having what others cannot have, or is it possible for you to still find pleasure in eating steak even when everybody can have it? Be honest now, you know that being richer than others is a source of pleasure, and you are not being blamed for this feeling; however, in your lifetime the purchasing power of many will always be greater or lesser than others even while the lowest level of mankind will be raised enormously, so you needn't concern yourself about this difference in wealth during your remaining years. Moreover, your millionaires are going to be given an opportunity of becoming billionaires, your thousandaires millionaires, and the poor people just wealthy. Now, once again, be perfectly honest. If I can show you how to invest your money (and labor) so that it will put to shame any investments you now have, and guarantee a fabulous return, would you be interested? Am I giving you a choice? Wouldn't you like to double and triple the value of your money and labor so that you can buy many of the luxuries you have only been dreaming about? Would it satisfy you to know that it will be mathematically impossible for your income to ever stop or decrease, although it will definitely increase enormously? To understand how this great transition comes about, it is necessary only to follow God's will, Thou Shall Not Blame, and observe in this book the mathematical relations which will compel each reader to desire changing himself into what he cannot deny, for he sees at last what is truly better for himself.

The inception of your Golden Age will actually get underway just as you launch a satellite into space, with a countdown, and when the count is down, every weapon will be destroyed, prisoners released and prisons demolished, and all the money will be burned or melted. It should be obvious that this countdown will not take place until every adult on your planet is taught what it means that man's will is not free, for otherwise it would only make matters worse. However, once this is accomplished and the project Golden Age is launched, millions upon millions of people will be automatically displaced as a consequence, but just before the launch, since no one can be blamed or hurt, each person around the planet will record in his little book his exact wealth and earning power. In other words, at the precise moment this project gets under way not one single penny in purchasing power will be taken away from any individual, regardless of whether or not he is displaced. Consequently, if the president of the United States, the premier of Russia, the queen of England, etc., have been receiving a net income of so much, they will continue to receive this same amount of money without anyone telling them what to do with their time or how to spend their money. If the sailors and soldiers returning home wish to retire for the rest of their lives on their present income, this is their business, but if they desire to earn more money, then they will be compelled of their own free will to desire going to work. Furthermore, each person will record in his book the exact amount of time he is putting in to earn his present income (this applies only to those employed) because it will be impossible for an individual to work one second longer without blame. Under these conditions, it is also impossible for inflation to set in, which means that the purchasing power of your dollar will never decrease. In other words, if number one is the richest man in the world, number two next, number three next, etc., until number 100 is the poorest, there will be no possibility of your purchasing power being affected by one group suddenly preventing another group from satisfying desires because of inflation. Let me clarify this another way.

If you have a desire to buy a Cadillac and only one is available, you will be given preference if your wealth is greater, but if two people apply with the same exact amount of wealth it is obvious that neither would desire what tacitly blames the desire of the other, and the only way such a situation could be equitably solved would be by tossing a coin providing the other individual can order a similar car. If the millionaires wanted to buy the more expensive items and suddenly discovered that it is impossible because everybody is now in a position to buy them, their purchasing power would be a mockery. But God is not going to let this happen, and here is how this is accomplished.

Planet Earth is going to be one gigantic corporation in which every individual who works or has money will buy stock in accordance with their wealth. If you are presently earning $100 per week net income (take-home pay), this will be added into the total, you will own a small fraction of this corporation, and you will share equitably in the total profits according to what fraction you own. If you prefer selling your investments from which you are deriving an income in order to have cash, you may do so, but this will not entitle you to a share in the corporation, nor will your income continue. In other words, if you are receiving six percent interest on $100,000, you could either keep the latter as cash on hand, which would be entered in your book, or else you would be guaranteed $6,000 a year for the rest of your life, less taxes, plus having this net amount entered as a share in the corporation. It is quite obvious which is the better investment on your part, giving you no choice, since $100,000 would not last too long. No one will determine for you what net income you derive from your investments, but whatever it is, you will submit this figure to your government, where it will be added to the total, and then to a grand total at the United Nations. You will also submit any investments you have from which you do not derive an income, so that your total stock in the corporation will receive an equitable share of the total profit. Remember, whatever your net income is at the time the transition gets underway, it will never be decreased because to do so would be blaming you for receiving too much money, although it definitely will be increased. Any cash on hand will be included as stock in the corporation. It should be obvious that any money owed to you, which is included as part of your investment, will be figured in your income, while the debtors will list the amount still owed as a deficit in their books. For example, if you are paying $120 per month on your mortgage, you will still continue to pay this amount by deducting the payments in your book, but the property will be yours because the bank will have already figured in what you owe in its profit and income. If you owe a collector salesman $100 for a refrigerator you will still owe this amount, and will pay it as you are supposed to because no one will ever blame you if you never pay back a dime; but the installment man will figure in the amount due as part of his income, while being displaced not only because any approach of a seller to a buyer is a form of tacit blame, but primarily because no salesmen are necessary on a cooperative planet. Another way of saying the same thing is this: your total assets, which include everything, your total income, your total liabilities, will buy a share of the corporation in accordance with what your purchasing power allows, but all your debts will be automatically wiped out without hurting your creditors because their stock in the corporation will be increased while the stock of the debtors will be proportionately decreased.

Under these conditions it makes no difference whether you buy in one store or another simply because you receive an equitable share of the total profit, and if you suddenly discover that you require additional help to handle the extra business so that no one's labor time is increased, all that is necessary is to advertise for it.

Now it is important to bear in mind that a displaced individual cannot deposit in the corporation the income he receives because this depends on the labor of others, although he can deposit any investments or cash he may have. For example, if the President of the United States desires to retire for the rest of his life on his present net income, he can do so without any form of tacit blame on his part. This applies to any individual who is displaced, but this income cannot be included as a share in the corporation. However, the people who have money and investments are not displaced, even though they may not be doing anything but lie on the beach all day. If a stockholder receives an income as a consequence of this money being invested, his income can be deposited as a share in the corporation because it still plays an active role in the economy, even though this individual can retire since there is nothing for him to do. Consequently, if any displaced individual receives an additional income from personal investments, he may deposit this, but not the income he receives from the labor of those who are supporting him. This is a very crucial point because it will compel a displaced person, whose income will soon fall below the rising level of the lowest paid worker, to desire getting a job, since it does not satisfy him to remain idle when he sees that his purchasing power can be increased by going back to work. Furthermore, it will be impossible for these displaced to desire going back to work just as long as the lowest income group of the working is below that of their own, which means that men like the President of the United States who are displaced with a substantial income will retire for the rest of their lives since it is impossible for them to desire going back to work when this would only mean a cut in their income when the rising level of the lowest paid is still beneath what they have been guaranteed. Let me clarify this while revealing God's infinite wisdom.

At the present time the differences in wealth are necessary and cannot be blamed, which means that a cut in the income of any individual by as much as one penny tacitly blames this person for receiving too much. However, how is it mathematically possible for any new worker, regardless of his training and education, to begin work with a higher salary than the lowest paid person presently working, without blaming the janitor (who shall represent the lowest paid) for being inferior? This is an extremely crucial point. Since it is impossible to pay a new worker, one who begins after the transition gets underway, a penny more than the lowest paid on Earth, without tacitly blaming this other as being inferior, God has given you no choice but to start every new worker, regardless of his training and education, at the same level. However, this level is going to rise at such a fast rate that these words lose all significance. Furthermore, every unemployed worker, at the time the transition begins, will be compelled to go to work before the displaced because their income is less or none at all. If a person is on relief, getting welfare or compensation of some sort, this amount will be his income, which will not be included as a share in the corporation, and if the income level of the lowest worker is below this compensation, the compensated will not desire to return to work until it reaches their level.

Regardless of how you obtained your income you will continue to receive the same amount when you are displaced, even if you are a gangster, politician, lawyer, etc., not because it is a form of tacit blame to stop it — although this allowed the perception of what is better for yourself — but only because the purchasing power of each individual plays a vital role in the economy. Once again, let me clarify so you can fully appreciate the great change every single individual on your planet will be compelled to prefer of his own free will.

It should be obvious that a steel mill is dependent on the manufacturer to keep its men employed, as the manufacturer is dependent on the wholesaler, the wholesaler on the retailer, and the retailer on the consumer — which is you. However, when your earning power does not permit you to buy back what is produced, innumerable items come to a standstill unless there are sufficient foreign markets or sufficient credit among the masses, which lays off millions of workers. Many wars resulted because of this keen competition in a foreign market, and at the present time, in the United States, consumption has slowed tremendously due to the fact that a saturation point is reached, whereby a merchant cannot risk any more credit to the masses. Consequently the United States is on the verge of a great depression which can only be solved in one of two ways — either war with the communist world which will decrease the population and keep everybody employed, or else by removing the possibility of war which includes the end of all authority and control; but this still requires as part of the solution that the purchasing power of the masses be increased.

Now, when the people on Earth suddenly realize that their income is secure, that it will never be decreased, there will be a great desire to buy the many things needed and wanted, which, since it is impossible to increase the labor of anybody without blame, will result in a tremendous need for immediate employment. In other words, the total amount of labor on our planet, plus your total investments and your total income, are actually the total expenses to run this gigantic corporation at the start of the transition. Your profit will be twofold — a decrease in labor and an increase in purchasing power. Since any spending above the operating expenses of labor will necessitate employment, every person who goes to work automatically increases your profit in the corporation because his labor creates something above the expense of operation. This knowledge will compel every individual to spend freely in order to increase the profit necessary for his own satisfaction. To meet this great demand, every person now unemployed will find employment either in the capacity of helping to satisfy increased purchasing power or helping to decrease the total amount of labor time, as will be the case with those displaced whose income is less than the lowest paid working group, which compels a desire to return to work in order to increase their purchasing power.

Each person who has a share in the corporation will know very simply how much his profit has increased by the fact that the total invested in the corporation will be published in the newspapers so that he can determine for himself what fraction of this whole belongs to him. If the total is 1000, and you have deposited one, all you have to do is divide the latter by the former, and you will arrive at the percent you own. Then, when the total profit is listed each day, week, or month, you can determine your share by dividing the total profit by your percent of the corporation. Since the lowest paid of the investors will be steadily receiving their share of the corporation, every new employee who goes to work will increase the level of his own income just by going to work, and the starting salary, which is increasing rapidly, will be constantly listed in the newspapers so that a new worker will know instantly what amount of income is his take home pay, but he will not have any share in the corporation which doesn't mean anything when the level of the lowest paid will soon equal the highest paid. Since it is impossible for the lowest paid workers to ever be increased above each other, millions upon millions will receive the exact same income which presents a problem, regardless of the fact that this level will be steadily rising. Remember, it is mathematically impossible for any shareholder in this corporation to compete with the purchasing power of someone who holds a larger share simply because their purchasing power will always rise at the same ratio as when the corporation was formed. If you own one percent of the corporation, and someone else owns one-half of one percent, no matter how much profit is made, you will always have that difference of greater purchasing power. In other words, the stratified position that will prevail on your planet at the start of the transition, insofar as purchasing power is concerned, will hold true until you die and even for a while afterwards. If you are now the wealthiest man in the world, you will remain this individual until you pass away. Should you have saved several million dollars in cash during your life, when it comes time to pass on this wealth it will be necessary for you to distribute this in an equitable manner to the members of your immediate family, because any discrimination is a form of tacit blame, and your knowledge that no one would ever blame you for this makes it impossible to consider. Besides, in the new world, everything that predisposed a preference for one heir over another will be removed. Consequently, if five million must be distributed among five heirs, each one will receive a million in cash, which would go into the corporation to increase the purchasing power of the five heirs. When the individuals with their million bequeath what is left of their fortune in an equitable manner, it won't take long before this wealth will be reduced to a negligible amount. Since every new worker is compelled to start off at the same income, when all those who are now stratified in different income levels die off, every individual on Earth will have the same exact purchasing power, and as the wealthy displaced die off, taxes will take a tremendous decrease.

At the time of death, all your investments in the corporation will be divided in an equitable manner among your heirs. Consequently, each person who dies takes leave of the corporation in the degree his estate is subdivided. If his heirs do not wish to go to work, this is their business, but should they decide to, their purchasing power will not only be that of everybody else who starts a job but will also include the wealth that was handed along.

The problem that arises as a consequence of the masses having the same purchasing power at the start of the transition centers on the fact that unless each of these individuals is granted the same right to buy what the others in the same group desire, somebody is being tacitly blamed. For example, if a mother puts on the dinner table only enough milk for one child when she has two, she is tacitly blaming the desire of one of her children. In other words, if 50 million people, with the same exact purchasing power want steak, and there are only enough for 25 million, how is it possible to give steak to any of them unless the other 25 million will be placed on order, and unless the first 25 million are determined in some equitable manner? However, this does not apply, as was mentioned, when the purchasing power is different. If a millionaire wishes to buy himself a yacht, his desire does not have to consider those whose purchasing power or income is less, but it must consider all those who desire a yacht also and who have the same purchasing ability. The solution is not first come first served, as this is a form of tacit blame, but to distribute what is desired and available in an equitable manner in accordance with purchasing power, while allowing the others to place their order. Consequently, there is only one possible solution to the economic problem.

Each item produced must be catalogued, from which you will place your order in accordance with what you need and desire, and you will be given the opportunity to satisfy your desires in accordance with your steadily increasing purchasing power. This information will then be sent to the United Nations' scientists and mathematicians, who will have innumerable assistants to classify this information according to your present income, which includes the lowest level. It would make no difference who you are, if you have any desire for material things that have never been satisfied, just submit what you want, regardless of what it is, so that all this material can be analyzed in accordance with labor available, machinery, distribution, highways, land, etc. It is obvious that those who are hungry, those who need clothes and shelter, are the poorest of all. Consequently, the first consideration of the United Nations' scientists is to determine the best possible way in which to feed the population of Earth, without denying anybody their purchasing power where eating habits are concerned. This necessitates determining how many of each item can be produced in what length of time, which then reveals how to proceed. If there is an adequate quantity of milk to supply those who ordered it, then no man is so poor that he cannot afford milk and this applies to everything that is ordered; but when the demand is greater than the supply then those who have greater purchasing power will be given preference, and if these are already satiated with a particular item then what is available for immediate delivery must be equitably distributed while those who did not get one will be given a date as to when delivery can be expected. Consequently, your purchasing power will not be determined in accordance with *dollars* but with what is available and with what can be produced, and your profit will be shown daily or weekly in the newspapers as you now consult the stock market, in terms of what you can buy. If you have been wanting to buy a diamond ring and a Cadillac, all you have to do is consult the newspapers, and when your order for these can be met without tacitly blaming another individual within your own purchasing group, then you will observe that your profit has increased. As another example, if 300 thousand people desire to see the World Series, but only 50,000 seats are available in a stratified position of value, it is obvious that the wealthiest 50,000 will be given preference, and of these, the wealthiest will be given their choice of seats, for otherwise their wealth would be but a mockery. Once the wealth of every individual is exactly the same — it won't take too long — then the 300,000 tickets would be divided into six slips of 50,000 each, and one of the six would be drawn. Then the park itself would be divided into areas, placed on other slips from which another drawing would take place, and those who will be able to go to the ball game will be announced according to number so and so. You must constantly bear in mind that no one is to blame for what presently exists; therefore, the purchasing power of each individual must be respected. However, you must also bear in mind that within a relatively short time, as a matter of mathematical necessity, the purchasing power of each individual will be equal, and when you fully understand what death is, you will know that the Golden Age, not just the inception, will belong to you — not your posterity.

Under these conditions, everyone will desire to go to work because he knows that each individual is working for him just as he is working for them, and he further knows that no one will ever blame him if he never goes to work. But remember, a displaced person is free to live out his life without ever going to work, and without one ounce of blame. Only when he sees that the lowest income level of the working has exceeded his own can he possibly desire to return to work. However, under a cooperative system as described, the lowest paid worker will be shortly worth in round figures $500 per week because innumerable items now available for every family were never purchased by the masses who were always underpaid out of necessity. Each catalog will contain your purchasing power code number after the items and services that cannot be purchased, which will be listed in a numerical index. If you cannot afford a butler, chauffeur, housekeeper, etc. (these services will vanish in due time), your number will be listed indicating that you are not wealthy enough for these services. However, if your number is not so listed then you can advertise for this kind of help. Your purchasing power, your income in other words, will be determined by the board of scientists, economists, mathematicians, and listed in the catalog your family will receive in terms of items that can and cannot be bought. Items like cars, homes, etc., the larger, more expensive items, will have a special code number alongside of your own, providing your wealth allows you to be considered in an equitable drawing to determine which members of your group will get these items first, which members next, etc. If there is enough electricity, gas, phones, radios, televisions, etc., then no one is so poor that they cannot afford these things, and if there are items that cannot go around, then preference will always be given to those whose stratified wealth must be respected; otherwise, they would be tacitly blamed and their wealth a sham. However, no individual can complain when nothing is taken away from him and he is granted complete freedom to do what he wants to do, which hurts no one since it is impossible to want to hurt another under these conditions.

Since there is no more competition, the car manufacturers, etc., will combine their efforts to produce what is truly superior because this will only shorten their labor time. The same with homes. If a house can be built to last for several centuries, then it will be handed along from generation to generation. If a car can be manufactured to last for ten, twenty, thirty years (soon 99 percent of all accidents will cease, as you will see very shortly), then the amount of labor will be reduced tremendously. The same holds true for clothes and all other items. Whereas before competition flooded the markets with cheap items, while many things went to waste, cooperation compels only the best to be manufactured because it reduces the labor time of everybody who wants to take off from work as soon as possible. With atomic energy available, it will only be a relatively short time before your needs and desires, as with us on Mars, will be satiated with material things, and then your leisure will be spent in games, just having fun doing what you want to do. What is the point of working if you do not have to? The fact that your labor time will be reduced to virtually nothing is the great incentive to producing all that is needed and desired as soon as possible. If you have a home, swimming pool, car, private plane, all the clothes you could possibly desire plus all the conveniences that could go into a house, what is there left to desire? In what you call 1950, we averaged 100 hours per individual per year in actual labor time, so we had plenty of leisure to travel, play games, and do many other things for satisfaction. How long do you think it would take your manufacturers around Earth to produce enough food for everybody, enough clothes, enough cars, enough of everything you want in your home, when the many millions now unemployed and displaced are compelled to desire going back to work in the new economy? How long do you think it would take for your engineers and scientists to redesign your planet in accordance with what is best for everybody: roads, highways, farming — and a piece of land on which each individual can have his home built when his number comes up. Naturally, if your wealth permits having a home built immediately or sooner than other groups, nothing will prevent you. All graves and cemeteries will soon be considered a waste of good land because death is truly a mirage, which will be explained shortly in mathematical language that no one will be able to deny. If you prefer selling your home and building another, this is your business, but everything will be determined in accordance with your purchasing power. You may be wealthy enough to own several homes, but again, this is your business, for which no one can be blamed.

Your project Golden Age cannot be launched in proper orbit until every adult on your planet fully understands what it means that man's will is not free, until your scientists and mathematicians make up this catalog in accordance with a code number for each purchasing group, and until your planet is redesigned in accordance with what is truly best for all mankind as a whole. Then you will be ready for your great launching at which time all the money, guns, ammunition, prisons, etc., will be destroyed without the slightest fear that something can go wrong and without the slightest disharmony. This can take place almost immediately when an all-out effort is made to teach the principles in this book.

God has purposely made your abilities different so that each person can fall into a particular group that enables the whole to function in a perfectly balanced mathematical equation, but this does not mean that one person is any better than another. You will be drawn to do (those who will be unemployed and displaced) the kind of work you know you can do well because mistakes you make will never be blamed, which compels you to avoid a situation that can give you no satisfaction. Consequently, when the various employers around your planet advertise for help, you will be drawn to do only what you know positively you can handle, not only because all starting income will be identical, but also because it would be painful to you to hurt the economy in some way for which you know you would never be blamed. Remember, if you are unemployed and do not wish to go to work but would like to build a mansion and have innumerable luxuries, nothing is preventing you from taking advantage of your freedom to hurt the economy this way — if you want to. But how is it possible to want to when you know that no one will ever question your purchasing power or blame what you do, since it is now known that you are compelled to do what you know you are not compelled to do if you don't want to.

When you apply for a job, you won't have to fill out any applications, you won't have to answer any questions, you will just be shown what is required on the job. Everybody will find employment because the labor of each person employed at the time of the transition can never be increased, only decreased. And all employers will be prevented from advertising for help unless absolutely necessary because they will know that no one will ever blame them for hurting the economy this way. Certainly, you can cheat if you want to, but how is it possible to want to when this will only hurt you, since it could never give you satisfaction under the new conditions of knowing that you will never be blamed.

The board of scientists will determine the age for retirement in accordance with various factors, and when an individual approaches that age, he will advertise his position for the purpose of drawing a replacement from the youth who have arrived at a working age. It is important to remember that whatever you are doing at the time the transition gets underway, providing you are not displaced, plays an active role in the economy, which means that if you left your position without getting a replacement, you would be hurting someone who would never blame you for this hurt, consequently freezing you to your job. But under the new conditions, it makes no difference what type of work you are presently doing, even if it's a butler, housekeeper, etc., because you will be receiving an equitable share of the profits that accrue to the corporation, and also because you will no longer be judged inferior due to your type of work.

If the scientists determine that the population on Earth is beginning to get crowded, they will announce this in the newspapers, and the very fact that you will never be blamed for this overcrowding, which hurts the economy, will compel you of your own free will to desire limiting your family in accordance with what is best for everyone. Science will actually govern Earth as it now governs Mars, but without telling one person what he must do. Socialism, communism, and capitalism dictate laws that must be obeyed or else, which was necessary up until the discovery that man's will is not free; but now you are completely free by the will of God to do anything you want to do without fear of being blamed, criticized, condemned, or punished in any way, which limits your freedom to do only what hurts no individual. Have you any conception of the enormous wisdom that governs this universe? Is it possible for you not to desire this kind of world? This does not depend on your President, Premier, or Queen to make the decision as to when to begin your great transition, but on how quickly you can understand what it means that man's will is not free, for the very moment the United Nations is ready, the countdown will begin, and Project Golden Age will be launched. This is not a theory, not a figment of the imagination, but a mathematical fact that must come about because it is what you, the people on Earth, really want; only your relations with each other have been so involved that the problem was impossible of solution without the knowledge that man's will is not free and what this means. Just as Christ was born to do a particular job as was Hitler, neither being any better than the other in view of the knowledge that man's will is not free, so was I called to this planet to also do a particular job, which is to help you get this project Golden Age launched in proper orbit. Consequently, when this book is published and translated, when the scientists recognize that the knowledge herein is undeniable, they will gather from all parts of the world, and plans will be made to launch what everybody has been unconsciously expecting and praying for since time immemorial. Who am I to speak so confidently? Just another individual obeying God's will, no better or worse than anyone else. Are you scientists and thinkers interested in bringing this knowledge to light? If you are, then please become part of the solution by getting this knowledge carefully investigated, for it is obvious that you earthlings have the power to prevent a war that could destroy millions upon millions of lives. If you are having a difficult time understanding what cannot be denied, then I suggest that you submit what is beyond your capacity to those who have the ability to grasp these undeniable relations. Remember, a chimpanzee doesn't understand that two plus two equals four, but this doesn't negate the validity of what is undeniable; so please bear in mind that you are not the judge of this book, just an individual trying to understand what is written in terms of its value to you. Consequently, if you understand these relations, you will be given no choice as to what you must do, which again reveals the infinite wisdom of God in accomplishing his will, which must be done. Remember, Earth was still round even when you thought it was flat.

As a consequence of knowing what it means that man's will is not free, all carelessness is automatically removed because to hurt someone who will not blame you for doing what you know could have been prevented had you not been careless, gives you no choice. Driving a car under these new conditions, unless you know what you are doing, is equivalent to playing with a loaded gun, and if you can get any satisfaction out of standing around while the parents weep over the death of their child just killed by you who will not be blamed or punished in any way, then, my friends, you will be able to do the impossible. Consequently, a great responsibility is placed upon the shoulders of anyone who has anything whatever to do with cars, and instead of being anxious to drive each person will be more anxious to make certain that he really knows how first.

In your present world the very fact that you carried insurance tacitly blamed and justified what nobody wanted. I met one man who had seven accidents in one year and was not the least bit concerned because he always had enough liability insurance to cover the damages; but now it is impossible to get insurance against hurting others, which means that your accident rate will virtually drop to zero, while your scientists will design crossings and playgrounds for children so that no possibility of an accident will occur because of the child who also can never be blamed.

When a plane crashes, it is the responsibility of all those who have anything to do with it: building, repairing, maintaining, piloting, etc. Consequently, when these individuals know that they will never be blamed for taking thousands of lives, they will never allow a plane to go up until they are certain that no one will be hurt. Everybody will be compelled to assume the responsibility of hurting others in these plane crashes simply because the others will never blame them for this hurt. Right now your mechanics, engineers, etc., are justified in being careless because they know that somebody is going to blame somebody, but when they know that nobody will ever blame anybody they will all feel the weight of a tremendous responsibility which compels them to ground a plane unless they can feel absolutely certain they are not sending a group of people to their death. The very fact that all competition will be removed permits research to move ahead at an enormous rate, and there is no reason why any airplanes should crash into each other when all planes can be electronically guided as to altitude and direction.

This knowledge that you will never be blamed for an accident will lessen the labor of automobile repair shops to such a degree that if and when one occurs, each individual would obviously be wealthy enough to have their own car repaired. However, repairing cars as a result of an accident will not be a problem as each person will be compelled to desire learning how to handle this loaded gun very skillfully, otherwise he will never desire to drive a car because the hurt is too great to himself when there exists a possibility of being responsible for killing someone for which he will be excused and prevented from justifying. Everything that happened in the past as a result of carelessness is compelled to leave your planet because you have no choice in this matter at all, when the knowledge that you will never be blamed for what you know could have been prevented had you wanted to is a tremendous source of dissatisfaction.

Your scientists will set up a perfect traffic system which you don't have to obey if you don't want to, but when you know that it is solely for your own good, since it will prevent you from hurting another, for which you will never be blamed, you are compelled to put the horse before the cart. Everything takes a reverse turn because everything was built on the foundation of free will. The wisdom here is so fantastic that it is no wonder men like Spinoza became God-intoxicated, which has nothing to do with religion, as you well know since he was excommunicated; but it is even more amazing when you realize that we ourselves are a part of God and that we have been endowed with the ability to foresee what is truly better for ourselves when compelled to look ahead as a group, not as single, isolated individuals. Under these conditions of what value is prayer anymore when your prayers are answered by obeying God's will — Thou Shall Not Blame? In other words, how is it humanly possible to desire hurting yourself when you are shown how to prevent it?

Obviously, the drivers of tomorrow will rarely sound their horns because everything that gave rise to this desire will be precluded by the advance knowledge that nothing will be blamed. A taxi driver will often write up his manifest at a stop light and not concern himself about the cars behind because he knows that sooner or later someone will blow a horn to tell him that the light has changed; but when he knows the people will never blow their horn no matter how much he hurts them with this delay, he can get no satisfaction out of being responsible for tying up traffic when he knows he can prevent it. Besides, he won't need to write up any more manifests.

In concluding this chapter just bear in mind that it is mathematically impossible for one nation or one individual to strike another when all tacit blame is removed, which compels a cooperative economic system to be born. Consequently, if the people on this planet are seriously interested in ending all war, crime, unemployment, poverty, etc., they are given no choice but to end all government since there is no solution to this problem otherwise. However, no one will be hurt during this transition because every income that now exists, regardless of what you are doing to earn a living, will continue even after you die. Whatever life insurance you are now carrying on yourself will go to increase the purchasing power of your survivors, but in actual reality, since your own income will continue less the amount you yourself required, the amount of insurance you now have is already figured in for your benefit. No one will be unmarried in the new world, so a man's income or his purchasing power will continue until his wife is deceased and his children married or working — same difference.

Bear in mind that money itself is a form of tacit blame, although it is not removed because of this, but only because it is a useless appendage when man is compelled of his own free will to be absolutely honest with himself and when everybody is working for him. How is it humanly possible to desire taking what belongs to another when you know this hurt will never be blamed, and when you also know that before very long, you will be just as wealthy as anyone else? Every individual who plays a role in the economy is just as important as anyone else, and the janitor or barber will be just as wealthy very shortly.

Millions upon millions of people now employed will be permanently displaced, such as lawyers, accountants, theologians, the government, salesmen, psychologists, employment agencies, credit investigators, collection agencies, crime investigators, the manufacturers of burglar alarms, locks, cash registers, money; all gangsters, racketeers, etc., who make their living by cheating people will also be displaced but will receive the exact income they are accustomed to getting, for in the eyes of God there is no discrimination since every individual was and is obeying his will.

Remember also that it is imperative for each person to keep his own records of his income and stock in the corporation, since no one henceforth will be concerned with your business. However, your actual purchasing power will be translated by the United Nations' scientists from dollars and cents into merchandise and services. Your total wealth, whatever it is at the time the transition begins, buys a percent of the corporation which does not include the income given to the displaced, unemployed, or new workers; but the new workers automatically share in the profits by the fact that the smallest shareholder is their starting salary, and his profit is steadily rising. Consequently, when these people go back to work in the new economy, your investment will double and triple itself in a very short time while decreasing your labor because the labor of every new worker is a profit which everyone shares in an absolutely equitable manner.

Now tell me, is it possible for the working man to be dissatisfied with the knowledge that he will have a steady income which will never decrease, only increase? Is it possible for the clergy and government to be dissatisfied with being given a permanent income while God accomplishes the very things they have been unsuccessfully trying to bring about? Can they be dissatisfied going on a permanent vacation with full pay, and with no one to tell them what to do? Can the millionaires be dissatisfied with the opportunity to invest their money in a corporation that will guarantee greater leisure and still greater wealth? Is it humanly possible for any country to be dissatisfied with what can only satisfy? For the very first time, you are getting an accurate glimpse of the tremendous ignorance that passed for knowledge, for which nobody is to blame.

It shouldn't be necessary to analyze every minute detail of your economic problem because it is very easy for each person to make himself happy when everyone is compelled to do what he knows is better for himself under conditions that preclude all possibility of hurting others in any way. This brings us to the new system of self-development where everyone will be given an equal opportunity of finding happiness.

CHAPTER 8 — Education

I t should be obvious at this juncture why the educational systems of the world will be changed when so many professions, businesses and occupations have been permanently displaced. Of what value is it to study to be a general, theologian, lawyer, salesman, office manager, accountant, criminal investigator, credit manager, etc., when this knowledge will have absolutely no value. To study these subjects under such conditions would be equivalent to desiring to expend this great effort on an island where there are so many other things you would be compelled to prefer doing with your time. However, there is one aspect of education that is quite humorous because most of the knowledge you accumulated was unconsciously used to impress other people, and this not only can be demonstrated but the desire for such knowledge will be prevented from arising in a mathematical manner completely beyond your control, although in the direction of greater satisfaction.

Many students are drawn to read Shakespeare not because they find any real enjoyment but because they know that a certain type of cultured individual prefers this reading material; therefore, to become cultured, one must prefer the various things that are associated with culture — good manners, good breeding, good books, good music, good this and good that. You have been compelled to judge what is better for someone else the very moment you express an opinion as to what you think is good. Consequently, every definition, unless it accurately describes reality, is a judgment of what is right, which means that your dictionaries will be completely revised in accordance with undeniable terminology only. How is it humanly possible to define education when everyone born acquires an education from that time forward? How is it possible to define culture, character, manners, etc., when these describe differences that do not exist? Certainly, you saw these differences when you projected the word upon a difference in substance, but when the word is compelled to leave, when the slide through which you saw these differences is removed, you will perceive only reality. It is exactly as with war and crime: by removing all tacit blame, which included the removal of government and arms, war and crime were immediately prevented; and by removing the pretty colored glass through which you saw kaleidoscopic differences favorable to yourself, everybody becomes mathematically equal; but how was this possible unless it was known that man's will is not free and what this means? Perhaps you can appreciate the humor of this a little more by my quoting Will Durant, who considered himself an expert in so many things, for which he cannot be blamed. He writes: "I believe that it is through reading, rather than through high school and college, that we at last acquire a 'liberal education.' Mr. Everett Dean Martin has admirably described the meaning of this term, and I warmly recommend his book to those who wish to know what it is to be mature. Today we think a man is educated if he can read the newspapers morning, noon and night; but though our colleges turn out graduates like so many standardized Fords every year, there is a visible dearth of real culture in our life; we are a nation with a hundred thousand schools, and hardly a dozen educated men.

"No wonder that Mr. Wells and others have questioned the use of a college education. This is pessimism exaggerated to make a point; but it is well that someone should check us up in our notion that the multiplication of schools and graduates can make us an intelligent people. Our schools and colleges have suffered severely from Spencer's conception of education as the adjustment of the individual to his environment" (Spencer was mathematically correct but Durant was compelled to criticize a relation he could not understand which made it appear that he knew more than Spencer since he was the critic); "it was a dead, mechanical definition, drawn from a mechanistic philosophy, and distasteful to every creative spirit. The result has been the conquest of our schools by mechanical and theoretical science, to the comparative exclusion of such 'useless' subjects as literature, history, philosophy and art. So we make good office-boys, good clerks, and good technicians, who, when their work-day is over, devour the pictorial press and crowd into theatres that show them forever the same love-scenes on the screen and the same anatomy on stage.

"This mechanical and 'practical' education produces partial, not total, men; it subordinates civilization to industry, biology to physics, taste and manners to wealth. But education should make a man complete; it should develop every creative power in him, and open his mind to all the enjoyable and instructive aspects of the world." (His world instead of "the world" makes all the difference in the world.) "A man who is heavy with millions, but to whom Beethoven or Corot or Hardy, or the glow of the autumn woods in the setting sun, is only sound and color signifying nothing, is merely the raw material of a man; half the world is closed to the blurred windows of his spirit. An education that is purely scientific makes a mere tool of its product; it leaves him a stranger to beauty, and gives him powers that are divorced from wisdom." (Words that have absolutely no true meaning whatever.) "It would have been better for the world if Spencer had never written on education.

It is well that Latin and Greek are passing from our colleges, for they consumed a hundred times more effort than they were worth. As Heine said: 'The Romans could not have had much time left to conquer the world if they had first had to learn Latin.' But though the languages of Greece and Rome are necessary only to philologists, the literature of these nations is almost indispensable to education. A man may conceivably ignore Virgil and Horace, Lucretius and Cicero, Tacitus and Marcus Aurelius, and still become mature; but of all possible instruments of education that I know, none is so fine and sure as a study of Greek life in all the varied scope of its democracy and imperialism, its oratory and drama, its poetry and history, its architecture and sculpture, its science and philosophy. Let a student absorb the life and letters of the Periclean age, the Renaissance, and the Enlightenment, and he will have a better education than any college can give him. Education does not mean that we have become certified experts in business, or mining, or botany, or journalism, or epistemology; it means that through the absorption of the moral, intellectual and esthetic inheritance of our race we have come to understand and control ourselves as well as the external world; that we have chosen the best as our associates both in spirit and in the flesh; that we have learned to add courtesy to culture, wisdom to knowledge, and forgiveness to understanding. When will our colleges produce such men?"

This reveals conclusively how unconsciously ignorant Durant was compelled to be as he obeyed the law that made him move in the direction he did. He saw thousands of differences with his very eyes, and no one would have been able to convince him that what he referred to as direct perception was only a projection of words upon the outside world. The greatest humor imaginable lies in the fact that, without doing any reading at all, those born in the new world surpass in every way what he describes as a mature individual. He never understood himself, or he would never have been able to write what he did, which indicates he had no real control over himself; he considers one person and one book better than another, although these are better for him. I read *The Decline and Fall of the Roman Empire* along with *The Story of Civilization*, and although I prefer the former, this does not make it better. The kind of courtesy he has in mind permits criticism which is prevented in the new world; as for culture, this obviously is only a judgment that certain people and certain pursuits have greater value than others, which is a wholly fallacious perception. As for wisdom, it was something Durant never understood or had because it is simply the perception of mathematical relations where human conduct is concerned. As for knowledge, this was something he possessed a great deal of, but how much of what he learned was true? And last but not least, forgiveness only reveals that he was judging again the actions of others; otherwise, no forgiveness would be necessary, and this was added to the understanding he never possessed.

Most of your philosophers spent a lifetime hovering directly over the meaning of wisdom — which is the knowledge that man's will is not free and what this means — and received unconscious incursions from this world below, which allowed them to sniff this delightful aroma of wisdom; but now everyone born can eat this delicious steak without having to go through a lifetime of tidbits. This is equivalent to a man who dreams of making passionate love, only to discover that when he gets married (in your present world), the passion disappears; but now everyone can have this passion all through their lives. Durant spent a lifetime reading and learning, which enabled him to earn a living by writing, but he was compelled to justify the expenditure of such great effort on the grounds that it made him into a better, finer, cultured person — only words.

These words contain a hidden fallacious standard that justified the judging of others in terms of this standard. As a consequence, you were allowed to put others down (in a logical manner) while elevating yourself. But again, the humor lies in the fact that those psychologists who knew this were constantly compelled to do what they criticized in others because they were unconscious of the differences. I heard a man say that he can't understand why a person who furnishes his home should be concerned about how others fix theirs; then, in the next breath, he said he couldn't understand how people can enjoy playing golf on Sunday in preference to what he found more enjoyable and was completely unaware of this ignorance. Did you know that every time you express an opinion, you are blaming everybody who disagrees, which means that when you say everyone is entitled to their opinion, you are judging the opposite view as false, which indicates that you are mathematically at fault, for which you are not being blamed. But the desire to express an opinion disappears when tacit blame is removed, because it is not necessary to express an opinion when everybody knows that two plus two equals four. Consequently, the conversations in the future are going to be quite different for various reasons.

At the present time someone will ask, "Do you know when Columbus discovered America?" and when you say you don't know the other will proceed to tell you, which indicates that had the questioner known positively that you knew the answer he could have gotten no satisfaction out of asking the question only because he would not have been granted an opportunity to reveal this difference which he considered a form of superiority. What could possibly be my motive in asking you to work out some mathematical problem unless by your not being able to do it you are lowered and I am raised; but when I am prevented from asking such a question there is no value in my possessing the kind of knowledge that cannot be aired, or the kind that only reveals my ignorance to others, unless there is a certain pleasure in working out mathematical problems or in learning when America was discovered, which brings me to another very crucial point in my book.

How is it possible to ask a question that tacitly blames the other for not answering unless you know that the other will desire to answer? You may ask all kinds of foolish questions for the purpose of raising your feeling of superiority. But when it is known that the person who asks a question strikes the first blow, then the one who is asked has a justifiable right to ignore any question that he doesn't like answering. In many cases, however, he would desire to answer so as not to make you look foolish in your own eyes. Consequently, unless you know that your question is of value and does not attempt to lower another, you had better not ask it because it would only reveal your ignorance. Under these conditions it would be impossible to ask the question about Columbus when you already know the answer because the only reason it could possibly be asked is to make the other individual feel inferior, which puts a mathematical end to all knowledge that exists only for the purpose of showing that you know something someone else doesn't know since it will now be considered the worse possible alternative. Furthermore, if I want to know when Columbus discovered America for some legitimate reason, how is it possible to ask unless I know you know, which doubt compels me to consult an encyclopedia so as not to tacitly blame your ignorance of the answer. Isn't it obvious that this information has value only in earning a living or showing off, but how can one show off when this necessitates making a fool of oneself?

Supposing a whole group of people were shipwrecked on an island, and among them was an individual who memorized every bit of knowledge in the entire world. He read every book, every encyclopedia, and could even recite *The Decline and Fall of the Roman Empire* while standing on his head. One day, he sees a group of tumblers showing off, for which everybody applauded, and he feels a great desire to show this group that he is the smartest man on all Earth, but how can he go about it? He begins by asking this one person what he did for a living, to which the reply is, "I'm a carpenter." But this carpenter doesn't return the question, which leaves it again up to our genius to make the others aware of just who he is. "Say, do you know when Columbus discovered America?" "No, I don't." "Well, it was back in 1492." "My friend," says the carpenter, "if you already knew the answer, what was your purpose in asking me the question?" "I was trying to reveal to everybody here that I am what people call the brain; there is no book I haven't read and absorbed and no question I can't answer. I just wanted to entertain everybody as the tumblers are doing." "My friend," says the carpenter, "these tumblers don't bother us with foolish questions; they just start tumbling, and if we don't like the entertainment, we can turn our backs and go to sleep without offending them in any way since we didn't ask them to start. However, we enjoy the tumbling, and that is why we are applauding. Do you see that gentleman over there? Well, he can stand on one finger, and when he does that stunt, everybody gets as close as possible to see how this amazing feat is accomplished; but if your entertainment involves us answering a lot of foolish questions, I'm afraid you had better go back home because your desire makes an imposition on our desires. However, you certainly can parade up and down mumbling when America was discovered without imposing on us, and you did say you can recite *The Decline and Fall of the Roman Empire* while standing on your head, which I would like to see because I heard of yogis that do similar feats like climbing flagpoles, looking at their navels for years, etc. You will get a lot of recognition for this feat, but of course that would require several months of your time standing on your head, and with this boat coming to rescue us I'm afraid we will have to postpone watching you, but perhaps one day we shall see you in a circus."

Are you beginning to see the immense humor and how much genuine ignorance passed for knowledge? How is it humanly possible to desire studying and memorizing certain things when it is impossible to use this information? This puts an end to the present method of teaching because the teachers are compelled to refrain from asking children questions the answers of which are already known to the teachers. Nothing gives greater rise to a false sense of superiority than this questioning of children, because everybody likes to teach them something. Just listen to this little boy's aunt, who is visiting her sister. "Jimmy, how do you spell Constantinople?" "C... O... N... I don't know." "Jimmy, you should know how to spell that word. Aren't you in the eighth grade now?" My friends, all this is compelled to take leave of your planet. Stop to weigh how many times you yourself have asked these foolish questions. Under these conditions, it is impossible for a married couple to ask, "Where would you like to go tonight, honey?" And then, when the answer is not to your satisfaction, you will suggest another place, which indicates that your question is an unconscious attempt to shift the responsibility of making the decision to your partner, who wonders why you ask when you could have stated where you wanted to go. But to do that would be selfish, so, not wanting to appear selfish, this kind of question is asked, which then allows you to disagree with your partner, who was tacitly blamed by your foolish question. Consequently, since neither partner in the new world can ask the other because the other would only say, "It's up to you, doll," since to state a place would tacitly blame the desire of the other, there is only one possible solution and that is for both to state on a piece of paper where they would like to go, put these in a hat, and the one that is drawn is the answer. The great humor lies in the fact that the husband and wife in the new world will always desire to make the other happy, which compels the husband to put on his slip where he knows his wife likes to go, while she will put on her slip where she knows he likes to go, just the opposite in your present world when you have been married for a little while.

As a further consequence of not being able to ask questions, the answers of which are already known to the questioner, all written and oral tests come to an end. So does homework, since it is impossible for the teacher to tell the student what to do. But there is one question that a teacher can ask a student without any blame, and that is, "Is there something you would like to learn?" The relation between a teacher and pupil is exactly like that between a salesperson in a store and a buyer. The buyer knows that the salesman is there to answer his questions and help him, but the salesperson can never be sure that the buyer is there to buy or just to look. The children are prevented from tacitly blaming the teachers or their parents by the questions they ask because it is what parents and teachers are primarily there for: to help the children who want help. But remember, it is perfectly all right to ask a child if he would like to learn something just as long as you are not imposing your desire as to what you think is right for this child, or what might be better called the end, not the means to an end he will select. Asking a child if he would like to learn how to tie his shoestrings is a means to greater comfort for the child, as is learning how to eat with a knife and fork, but to ask a child if he would like to learn how to play the piano, or if he would like to listen to classical music, is imposing the end you feel is better for the child. Once this difference is understood, you won't have any problem with your children because they will be compelled to move constantly in the direction of greater happiness.

This reveals that unless a subject is directly related to earning a living, or unless there is specific pleasure in reading something for its own sake, it is compelled to take leave of your planet since there would be no satisfaction for a weightlifter to spend his life developing huge muscles if he were placed on an island where nobody could ever see his body. What is the advantage of having a whole bunch of useless information you can't use? How is it possible for the exertion to be worth it? What are you going to do with the knowledge of when Columbus discovered America? If I am interested in getting information the only safe place for me to go where I know it won't be tacit blame to ask these questions is to school or to the library, which means that your knowledge of certain subjects will be used only in the capacity of a teacher, and what you continue to teach will not depend on someone judging what is right for children, but on the children determining what is better for themselves.

Psychiatry and psychology will be completely displaced, not only because there will be no possibility of anyone ever becoming mentally disturbed again, but also because the doctors will be prevented from taking advantage of their patients' ignorance, which heretofore has hurt many individuals with justifiable impunity.

At the present time a doctor is guaranteed the right to open an office and charge a fee to anyone who consults him providing he has completed what the school judges is important for him to know; but when all judging ceases, when the doctor has to determine for himself whether he is qualified, he is not too anxious to assume the risk of hurting someone which can no more be justified by saying this is what I was taught in school, because the teachers in the universities will go only by facts, not fiction, and if a doctor learns that what he has been taught is mathematically undeniable then he need not be afraid of hurting another, but it is impossible for anyone to know what takes place within a body that has the amazing power to adjust to most conditions, even those imposed by the medicines of the doctors. Their reputation doesn't originate in accurate knowledge but in the fact that there are those called quacks, in the fact that you fear getting worse unless you abide by their prescription, which elevates the value of the doctors, and in the fact that it is assumed a doctor knows what is better for the patient. Because you get well after swallowing all kinds of medicine, or because you are able to overcome certain fears after consulting a psychiatrist for years, does not prove the doctor is responsible for your recovery. In fact, the very moment your doctors desist from practicing, you will discover that most of your sickness has been the result of their profound ignorance, for which they cannot be blamed. He is out there to make a living just like anybody else, and when you tell him that you aren't feeling well he will prescribe something in order to get paid, and will justify many diagnoses on the grounds that there are people to whom he only prescribes placebos, which is equivalent to a surgeon justifying the removal of tonsils on the grounds that he doesn't remove everybody's. But when an individual leaves a university in the future, it will not depend on any graduation, but on whether he thinks he is ready for his chosen occupation. Bear in mind that the very fact every new worker must begin at the bottom of the ladder, which has no significance when the purchasing power has risen far above what you know, places all the emphasis in one direction only — what each person likes to do, and what each person will like to do is what he can do best; but what a child will be able to study for a living will be limited by the requirements of your gigantic corporation, and he will be prevented from doing anything that risks hurting another also because there will be no financial reward to the risk.

Under the new conditions, a doctor will be prevented from prescribing medicine, or diagnosing that an operation is necessary unless he is absolutely certain he knows what he is doing, because should a patient be hurt in any way as a consequence of his ignorance, he knows he will never be blamed for this hurt or make any more money. Strange as this may sound to your ears 90 percent of the people who have been treated by doctors got well in spite, not because of the treatment; and how many were killed and crippled with impunity, for which these doctors are not to blame in any way, would amaze you, but all this was necessary to learn what was learned about the body. Much good resulted to balance the hurt, but when you understand that you will always be here on Earth, that death is only a mirage of confused words in logical, not mathematical relation, then you will begin to fully grasp the enormous wisdom of God who kept you from knowing this until now.

Furthermore, much so-called sickness resulted from a preference to take a swallow of medicine to justify getting out of doing something distasteful. Millions of people get sick every year in order to take advantage of their sick leave, and millions of children will get sick to stay home from school. "I don't feel good" means "I'd better see a doctor." Consequently, when every individual knows he can stay home for as long as he likes without anyone ever blaming him, it is impossible to get sick as you know the word. God gave you a mathematical standard to determine whether or not you are sick, and that is your temperature, which is necessary to generate the heat required to fight off what is disturbing the body, but this doesn't mean something should be done. One boy cut his finger on a can; the mother rushed him to a hospital where he was given a tetanus shot, and that evening he came down with a high fever. The family doctor was called in, and the boy was put on a rigorous regimen of medicine. Only God knows how much sickness is the result of a doctor's ignorance, but *you* will know soon enough. Doctors and dentists both use fallacious standards to justify earning a living for which they cannot be blamed, as when a dentist recommends that teeth be straightened. But when a student is not told what is right and what is wrong unless the knowledge is absolutely undeniable, he is compelled to do research; he is compelled to find out for himself, whereas before, the pride you had in your degrees and your professional rank was the arbiter of truth. Just the other day, I heard an announcement warning people against buying health foods without consulting their doctor first, which puts the doctor in a position of being very important, more so than those who sell health foods. In the future, however, no one will be able to desire anything that could possibly hurt another simply because it doesn't increase his profit one iota, let alone the fact that he would not be blamed for this hurt. I also heard the other day an announcement that a periodic checkup every six months is advisable, which is justified on the grounds that an ounce of prevention is worth a pound of cure; but what is going to be prevented? The doctor is interested in one thing, and it is not your health, for which he cannot be blamed, since everybody is under the compulsion of earning a living, though not anymore. This does not mean that he wouldn't like to be responsible for making you well when you're ill, because this is a tremendous source of satisfaction, as it satisfies a salesman to see people deriving pleasure out of something he sold them. The primary concern of the salesman and doctor, however, is to have an income, but whereas the former doesn't, the latter does need a different kind of justification because the one is supposed to have higher ethical standards, which necessitates it in the world of free will. Let us examine some of the changes that must come about in the new school system of the future.

First, it is impossible to tell a child to go to school without tacitly blaming. Therefore, all authority and control are removed, as you know these, but children can be controlled very easily. Remember, the teachers want to run an orderly school, not a madhouse, and the desires of the teachers are involved also. Consequently, a time schedule will continue since the teachers feel this is better for themselves. However, the teachers will explain to all those who can understand, exactly what it means that man's will is not free, and when this is accomplished, each child will know that if he is late for a class, it will be impossible for him to interrupt what these children want to learn because he will never be blamed even though his late interruption is an annoyance. Obviously, any child who wants to learn will be compelled to be on time only because his desire will not be satisfied when he has to delay learning what interests him. He knows that his mother will never wake him, so if he is anxious to be on time before the class begins, he will have to set an alarm clock, and the manufacturers of these clocks will be assuming a tremendous responsibility, for millions of people will be hurt every day should these alarms be defective, for which no one will be blamed.

If a child is too young to understand what it means that man's will is not free, and for one reason or another hurts other children or the teachers in any way, he will be given a simple choice — either to stop hurting others or to stay home from school, which will be a terrible form of punishment when he sees all the fun children are having once all tacit blame is removed. This method of punishment will only be necessary at the outset of your transition because these habits were developed over the years. However, the immediate change will prevent 99 percent of all possible hurt, even here, since the children will see that nobody wants to hurt them.

When it comes time to start a child in school, there is no set age, provided no extra burden is placed on the teachers, and the parents must consider what is better for themselves as well as the child. He will be shown the fun that other children are having so that his desire can be aroused for this means to an end he himself will eventually select. Then the parents will ask him if he would like to go. Once he starts, no teacher will ever remark about how pretty someone is, cute or smart, for these words only develop fallacious slides through which a distorted version of reality is seen. Absolutely no records will be kept on this child as to his progress, for this imposes the fallacious standards of another's values, and before any inoculations are given, the doctors must be absolutely certain they know what they are doing, because no one will blame them for their ignorance. When you circumcise a baby, you are hurting that infant who cries from this hurt, and unless you can prove to yourself in a mathematical manner that this operation is better for the child, you will be compelled to forego the foreskin. The Jews developed this ritual from their ancient past, and because superstitious reasons only revealed ignorance, it was justified on the grounds that it was healthier; but why is it healthier? We have no circumcision on Mars, no disease, no sickness, no cancer, only healthy and happy people. The moment all of you fully understand what it means that man's will is not free, 99 percent of what now disturbs your body will be warded off because of the perfect condition of your mind, and strange as this may seem, many of your sicknesses are nothing but words which Montaigne and other philosophers perceived. Ninety-nine percent of what psychiatry treats are words, and the increase in mental patients can be easily traced to psychiatrists themselves, who unconsciously multiplied the heads of this diseased hydra by tacitly blaming the possibility of mental sickness, which justified and drove many to consider themselves in need of what must have come into existence for their welfare.

It is unimportant for the teachers to concern themselves about the talents of any child because this is not the business of anybody but that child. God is determined to see that every baby born, regardless of his race, color, or creed (insignificant words) will be given an equal opportunity of finding happiness. Consequently, there are no more men of Gold as Plato thought. If Einstein is among these children and is left alone, he will be drawn to science as a fish is to water, but this is his business, not that of his teachers or parents, and he will not be considered one ounce more valuable than another. All the teachers have to do is teach what the children want to learn and let them engage in competitive activities which are not an end such as spelling bees and tests about history, geography, grammar, etc., but a means to an end. The children will be shown all the various ways in which a person could become famous and then asked if they would like to become renowned in any particular field. Then the competition will begin right around your planet.

No child will be compelled to engage in any activity unless he wants to, but every game possible will be designed to test the mettle of each individual in competition with others, for this is the only way man gets to know himself and what makes him happier to do. If ten children, for example, would like to be a famous track and field star, then they will desire to compete against each other. The losers, of their own free will, will desire to look for some other means of becoming famous, but when no one blames these individuals for losing, even though everyone applauds the winner, they will be helped, not hurt, because they will see themselves as they really are. Since it is impossible for them to find satisfaction in losing, they will search for the activity in which they can succeed, and if they cannot find any, then they will desist from competition. However, innumerable games can be enjoyed when the competition is evenly matched. Many fields do not require competition to become famous, such as music, and if a child discovers a pleasure in listening to a particular type of music, or playing a particular instrument in preference to others, there will be nothing to hold back the development of any child to do what makes him happy.

The whole purpose of the educational system up until the time a child selects for himself the manner in which he will earn a living, is to give him an opportunity to see everything that exists, give him an opportunity to develop his skills (all incomes will be the same so money can never be the motive anymore which drew many parents to make decisions for their children), and allow him to work at a job he prefers. This places a great responsibility on your board of scientists to determine what population is required at each level of your growth to meet all the conditions of perfect harmony, which must take into consideration how much labor is required to meet the gradually decreasing demand of consumption so that each individual who is ready to retire can find for himself a necessary replacement. Consequently, the retirement age will be determined by the board of scientists in accordance with many factors, and every child who leaves school to go to work will automatically retire some individual.

Unless a male who graduates from school contributes to production, distribution, the various services, entertainment, or scientific research and development, he will know that he is a burden to society, for which no one will ever blame him. Consequently, he will be prevented from taking advantage of his freedom because there is no advantage to hurting others who will never blame him for this hurt.

There will be no more graduations because this is a fallacious, unmathematical standard that blames those who are now able to judge their own success and failure, but there will be tremendous competition among those, for example, who want to be an electrical engineer when only so many are needed. Those who fall by the wayside when a coin is flipped will be compelled to look for something else, but no matter what is decided upon, it can never be considered inferior to any other job because no one is judged anymore in terms of gold, silver, or bronze, and all positions pay the same salary.

Some people can do things better than others, but this does not make them better, and when a child understands what it means that man's will is not free, he will know instantly that applause for another is in no way a discredit to himself. Consequently, children cannot be allowed to engage in competition until they are taught the principles in this book; otherwise, your applause will hurt the loser.

The very fact that your school system passed everybody along from grade to grade was responsible for innumerable fallacious standards that justified the existence of ignorance, which passed for knowledge, simply because it was assumed that when a certain grade was reached, you were more educated than a person who didn't go as far as you. This allowed your professors, your Ph.D.s to be filled with pride over absolutely nothing, and they were resented by men like Edward Gibbon, Will Durant, and many others who discovered themselves superior by another fallacious standard. Everybody was judging by some standard which they felt was the truth, and all were entangled in words.

Spelling and grammar will be absolutely displaced because there is no value to either one. You learn both from reading and when you take pride in the fact that the 'e' in grateful should be after the 't' rather than before the 'a' only indicates to what extent you are truly ignorant, since both are correct when the meaning is obviously clear in the context and sound of the word. You make an issue of 'you and I' or 'you and me' as if this reveals anything but your ignorance. This is equivalent to the card player who insists that the cards be cut by the player on his right. Why? Because that's the way it is done. Furthermore, the very knowledge that you will never be blamed or praised for writing what no one can understand compels a writer to be absolutely certain his words are accurate.

Correct punctuation and good writing is being understood, nothing else; and if you read enough and realize that a comma is a pause, who is to tell you where to pause when each individual speaks differently. If you are understood when you speak, then you will be understood when you write, provided you write like you speak. However, sentences are equivalent to phrases in music and the punctuation helps you understand and appreciate the sentence as a whole, but this is learned very simply from reading and listening, not from studying grammar. Spelling is a waste of time and teaches a child to be proud of nothing, which is equivalent to dancing for joy because a child spells a word properly. Children don't spell when they speak, and they never make a mistake in spelling when they talk. The only time it paid to learn how to spell was in your world of free will when you were being judged at every turn. If I should write, "I am greatful for what you did," and you criticize this, what are you doing but using spelling to reveal what you feel is an expression of your superiority, although in actual reality you are only demonstrating your unconscious ignorance. The desire to spell accurately will arise from a desire to be understood, but the sentence above cannot possibly be misunderstood. Consequently, the dictionary would show either spelling as correct.

When a child enters school, he will never be taught spelling and grammar, which would be equivalent to teaching how to talk, but will be asked if he would like to learn reading, writing, and arithmetic, for these are means to an end, not an end as is grammar or spelling. Even if you never explained a comma, semi-colon, colon, period, the child would understand their meaning because he will identify them with the pauses in his own speaking; but if a child doesn't understand what you are trying to teach, you will need to improve your communication skills because everything, if explained properly with no effort to appear superior with big words, can be easily taught with clarity. Arithmetic is so easy to teach that a three-year-old could be taught, if taught properly, but instead you teach a child to remember rather than think. Give your average college student a mathematical problem, and he tries to remember what he was taught, not realizing that the answer doesn't lie in the method but in perceiving the relations. Algebra can make very difficult what is simple to understand if explained properly, as many of your philosophers have taken a simple truth that could have been explained in very few words and then made a profound book out of it that nobody understood, all because they judged the value of the book by the quantity of big words and the difficulty of being grasped. God knows how many poets, philosophers, psychiatrists, and psychologists have been accorded fame because someone imparted his own meaning, which to him was a confirmation of wisdom. To agree with a famous person is an unconscious way of saying I am as smart as he is; only he got a lucky break or is able to express himself better. Aristotle stopped the world from thinking for a while because everybody agreed with what he had to say, but what would he have to say about this book? How many of you recognized in Durant's Mansions of Philosophy your own wisdom, which now turns out to be ignorance? Another way of building up your own feeling of superiority is by disagreeing, but the great humor lies in the fact that the standards by which each of you judged the other were equally fallacious. Because 6 is closer to the answer of the cow problem than 7 doesn't make it less wrong, nor does a book like Dianetics become more true because it is dedicated to Durant, or less true because it was not accepted by psychiatry.

There can be absolutely no pleasure in reading history unless you have a motive in learning about the past, and what could possibly motivate what is not a pleasure in itself? In your present world you read to accumulate information, a large vocabulary, etc., so that this would distinguish you from others, but when this reveals your ignorance when you try to set yourself up as superior because of this difference, then you are given no choice but to forgo any great effort to acquire knowledge unless there is a pleasure which in no way hurts another person.

Geography also can have no appeal, for there is no way this information can be used except by those who need this knowledge for work, or unless you derive pleasure in accumulating useless information. As for philosophy and psychology, they will be relics of the past, and so will every book that is difficult to understand because no one will read it. The only reason many books continue in existence is because the teachers found keen satisfaction in raising their ego by imposing these deeper, hidden meanings on students. When the teachers are compelled to wait for the students, thousands of books will die a sudden death. Can you see what is happening to your educational system?

If children want to learn about the past, they can find much more enjoyment from stories, pictures, etc., than from reading the kind of material that requires great effort. And are they given a choice when it is impossible to use this knowledge or to ask a question the answer of which they already know, which shipwrecks each person with that kind of information on an island all by himself?

The new schools will have huge playgrounds, swimming pools, and every conceivable kind of game, toy, and entertainment. No one will have to read or study unless he wants to, and when it comes time to choose what he wishes to do for a living, which is really humorous because in a short time there won't be that much to do although he will want to be specifically trained, he will look over the many type jobs available and will be able to determine what he prefers through an elimination process which allows him to test and become accurately acquainted with himself. If one hundred apply for a position that calls for fifty, then an equitable manner of selection will be devised while in school.

The schools will teach girls how to prepare the tastiest meals, and when they reach the age of nubility, they will even be taught, if they want to learn, the many ways to arouse the passion of someone without physical contact and how to arouse passion still more after contact. There will be no shame in these classes for girls and boys, because when they are ready to get married all that is necessary is for a girl to attract the boy she wants for her husband, or vice versa, and she can do anything she wants to arouse his desire to take her out — without any harm and without any fear of being hurt. The boys, knowing this, will be compelled to avoid any girl who doesn't appeal, which will tell her immediately to find someone else. Since earning a living will not be a problem, these boys will desire to get married very young, not so much because of this, but because they will want to make love, and to do so they must get married since they have no other choice. Obviously, they could leave each other if they wanted to, but under the changed conditions, leaving would be impossible to prefer. Please remember that the word marriage in this context has nothing to do with legalities.

The world of entertainment will draw millions of professionals and amateurs, and television will be a major source of pleasure, but no one will judge whether you qualify to entertain; you must make this decision for yourself, and only if there is a need for entertainers. The newspapers and universities will list all the vacancies available. The very fact that money will not be a motive compels only the extremely confident to enter the world of entertainment on a professional basis because there is a risk involved in the fact that you may not be qualified which means that you are hurting the economy by being paid for a service that is of no value, for which you know you will never be blamed. However, everybody will be given the opportunity to entertain if they feel they have the ability, as the tumblers did on our island, but they will not be able to blame the audience for leaving or turning their backs. Consequently, this prevents the unskilled and untalented from entering the world of sports and entertainment, which compels the audience to applaud all efforts to entertain them. Are you beginning to see the wisdom? Had our genius on the island been aware of the knowledge that man's will is not free and what this means he could never have desired to entertain by asking ridiculous questions or reciting dates and events because the applause would have made him feel like an absolute fool, but to stand on his head while reciting a lengthy book does not impose on anyone and would be even more difficult a thing to do than standing on one finger while hoops are twirled with the feet.

All individual entertainment, such as singing, dancing, and acrobatics, can be done by anyone who consults the openings in each television studio, theater, or nightclub for the time available, and lists his name. Where group efforts are concerned you will consult the newspapers that list all openings, and where competition and winning as a team is involved, which places a tremendous responsibility on your ability when no one will judge it but you, and never blame you for weakening the team, you will also consult the newspaper, but when several applications are mailed in from different parts of the world to join a team that has an opening there will be no discrimination in selecting an applicant because all would have to be extremely qualified under the conditions, and flipping a coin would suffice. As to how many teams there should be in the various sports, this can easily be determined by the space and time available. In the future, there will always be something going on, and no one will be lacking for entertainment.

Education as you know it is a real farce under these conditions because there is not the slightest bit of difference in value between you, no matter what you choose for a living. The pride you now experience because of your education, your looks, your clothes, your wealth, your ability, completely disappears, although you will derive great pleasure in making others happy because this is a tremendous source of satisfaction. Under these conditions, only the people with absolutely fantastic abilities will desire to seek fame because there is nothing other than this denial of their talents that could be a source of dissatisfaction when each person is treated with the same exact consideration and respect. Many children and adults were driven to try almost anything to gain some recognition as another human being because your constant judging of how others should be compelled a search for isolated groups that paid each other the compliments desperately needed. But there was a purpose to everything because, strange as this may seem, each and every individual that ever lived and will live was always at the exact spot at the time he was supposed to be. All of us, no matter what we ever do, will always be cogs in the little wheel of our father or this immense universe.

In concluding this chapter, it is important to remember that any question is a form of tacit blame which strikes the first blow by judging that the other person desires to answer Since I cannot be blamed for not answering questions that are obviously foolish and are designed to hurt me by revealing that I didn't know as much, you are prevented from making a fool of yourself which knowledge compels me to answer all your questions so as not to hurt you. And this, my friends, makes it absolutely impossible to derive any satisfaction out of learning what can never reveal your superiority except where there is competitive activity and a mathematical standard; unless the knowledge you gain is the source of your income; or unless studying grammar, history, geography, literature, spelling, etc., is a source of pleasure in itself. This completely revolutionizes your educational system since the opinion of others, now removed once and for all, can no longer be an influence when no one henceforth will ever desire to judge what is right for you.

PART FOUR

The extension of a mathematical relation into the world beyond death

CHAPTER 9 — God and Immortality

CHAPTER 9 — God and Immortality

Doesn't it seem strange to you that of all the millions of years Earth has been in existence, you, of all people, should be born at this time to see the wonders of the world and the inception of the Golden Age? Why weren't you born back in the time of Socrates, or why shouldn't you be born a little later so that you could be around for all the fun when your scientists visit us on Mars? You older people who know that death is near, who have lost many loved ones, cannot help but think about what Durant referred to as the Great Enemy because you see and cannot deny that when someone gets buried in the ground, he never rises again, except in your imagination, as did Christ into heaven. Theologians and other philosophers received intuitive incursions that man was truly immortal, but they had no way of communicating or translating their feelings into language, which could not be denied because they were completely confused with words and beliefs.

But the problem is not so difficult when it is realized that your words have been fallacious symbols which prevented you from seeing the mathematical relations that no one can deny. For example, how is it humanly possible for you to have a choice when you are compelled to move in the direction

237

of satisfaction? These are easy relations to perceive once the truth is known about yourself. By the same reasoning (and here lies a great fallacy that was never completely understood), how is it humanly possible for there to be such a thing as the past and future when all we ever have is the present? Do you ever sleep in the past? Does the sun ever shine in the past? Is it possible for you to do anything in the past? Yet you have a word to describe something that has no existence in the real world. You use words like beginning and end, apply this to the universe, and think you are perceiving mathematical relations. You say God is the first cause, and reason from here as if you are discussing reality. But yet there are innumerable relations which cannot be denied once they are understood.

The word "past" is obviously the perception of a relation that appears undeniable because it has reference to the revolution of Earth on its axis in relation to the sun. You are conscious that it takes a certain length of time to do anything, and by also being conscious of space, you perceive that as you traverse a point from *here* to *there*, what is left behind as you travel is called the past, and your destination is the future. But in actual reality, you are not moving between two points, a beginning and an end, just in motion in the present. Socrates didn't live in the past; he lived in the present because there is no such thing as the past. The reason we say that Socrates lived in the past is because the particular individual is no longer here, but is it possible for you to say that God or the sun existed in the past? By perceiving things that are born and die, and by not understanding the underlying substance, a fallacious relation develops, which can easily be clarified once the word symbols are understood.

The great confusion centers around the fact that man is not conscious that his consciousness, through which he perceives his own individuality, is not an individual characteristic. Your particular face and body are individual things perceived by your consciousness of differences, and these differences perish and die, which cannot be denied. But your consciousness (and here's the key to the problem) never dies because it is the ability of the human brain to perceive relations which reveal the consciousness of individuality, and this consciousness, which is you at this moment of time, is passed along from generation to generation in the form of an unborn or potential mind. Let me clarify this.

Supposing we let A represent all the sperm in the entire world and B all the ova pertaining to mankind, while the combination of one with the other will be designated C, which is you. Now, supposing A joins up with B, and during their uterine journey, you, C, end up as a miscarriage; but your mother and father still want you, and they try again. This time, however, you are born, but 67 years later, you end up in a hospital where you die. Now think very carefully; is there any difference between the death of you in the uterus or the death of you 67 years later? Yes, you might reply, the first 'you' was not you, it was someone else with an entirely different heredity. Well, supposing the second 'you' didn't die in 67 years but immediately after birth, when taking a good look at the world; but mom and dad having a lot of fun trying, even though not successful, try a third time with success. Now, in actual reality, though hereditary differences exist between the three C's, the word you is a designation only for the viable substance which comes into the world and is identified with a name to establish these differences that mom and dad grow to love. But what is the difference between the you who dies immediately upon birth after having a heart attack upon seeing the world, or the you who dies 67 years later? Because you are conscious of your existence and individuality during those years in the present, write a book, build a home, make a lot of friends who cry when you die, doesn't take away from the fact that you are a combination of A and B, which continues in existence regardless of what happens to C. If you had died a hundred thousand times in the uterus of somebody, eventually you, which is a word describing the consciousness of differences about yourself, would have been born because you are also any combination of A and B, which continues in existence from generation to generation with a potential brain that is capable of consciously perceiving the differences of individuality about yourself. Consequently the consciousness you feel, the knowledge of your individuality without understanding that you, this individual person is not only C which represents the hereditary differences that die, but A and B which never die, because they are carried along from generation to generation and when united develop into the potential consciousness of individuality belonging to any C, makes you perceive an improper relation for you have not considered undeniable facts. Just because the entelechy of A and B develops into the consciousness of C, which permits the recognition of individuality, does not negate the substance from which C is derived. Even if all the individual characteristics lie potential in the germplasm, this still has nothing to do with consciousness, which is not an individual characteristic like your face. The word 'I' not only reveals these individual differences between yourself and others but also your consciousness of these differences. Now observe this mathematical reasoning.

Since there is no such thing as the past (this has already been established), there is only the present. Since it is utterly impossible for consciousness to ever exist in the past, for there is no such thing, it can only exist in the present. Since consciousness can only mean your consciousness, and this world exists only in the present, it is perceived during every moment of time through your consciousness, which, as that which lies potential in the germplasm of A and B, is always here when the combination of C develops into viable or conscious substance that perceives individuality. To say that a dead person is not conscious is absolutely true... but you are, and this perception that death is not conscious fails to consider more vital relations. The important thing that cannot be denied is this: Though death is obviously not conscious, the life in man is, and this feeling of consciousness can only be yours, regardless of how many live or die around you. Consequently since there is no such thing as the past, and consciousness can only be your consciousness (never that of another) which can only exist in the present, your consciousness, *not your body*, will always be here during every moment of time because it is not a personal attribute like the shape of your face, but that which applies to the living substance of all mankind and is given each person upon his birth enabling the perception of his individuality. Hereditary differences are personal characteristics that permit development but not consciousness, even though it perceives these differences, for this is an eternal attribute of God or this universe in its entirety, like space, time, and substance.

Now the protoplasm of all life exists as the living substance (A and B) from which all forms of life derive, and you (A, B, and C) are not the end result but a conscious development from this protoplasm. This I or ego that you feel is definitely a reality, for it is you, no one else, that tastes, touches, smells, hears, and sees. But this I or ego of consciousness is actually not an individual thing like the various differences about yourself that you have considered C, for it only exists, like space and time, as a perception of relations and is contained in the germinal substance of mankind as an eternal attribute of God, this universe in its entirety. Space, time, and consciousness are actually one and the same thing expressed differently, like two plus two, three plus one, and one plus one plus one plus one. Space and time are necessary prerequisites for consciousness, and consciousness is a necessary prerequisite for space and time, and all depend for their existence on the perception of relations, which ability to do so is contained in the potential of man's brain.

Now this potential ego or self-consciousness of God, who, as this entire universe, never dies because space, time, substance, and consciousness are always here, and this germinal substance containing the ability to perceive these relations is passed along from generation to generation, completely beyond the control of man. Since this germinal substance is that from which your ego, the feel of yourself as an individual, is composed, and since this I or ego that you feel is also the conscious expression of this germinal substance, both are one and the same thing. Consequently, the consciousness of all mankind is the ego or I of the germinal substance which imparts individuality upon the birth of a child, as a tree does to a leaf in the spring of the year. But this all-pervasive consciousness, which exists always in the present (and here is the solution), can only be *your* consciousness of another, for if it were possible to see this universe through the consciousness of someone else, you would be made king of all creation.

This all-pervasive consciousness can only be your consciousness because you are an individual expression of God's consciousness, which pervades the universe and continues to exist in the potential of a protoplasmic state. Consequently, each child born comes into the world with this I or ego, which, since it is just an individual expression of the germinal or protoplasmic ego, continues to exist after the body dies, and the very moment after death, his ego, the feel of himself as an individual existing that has never died because it exists as the potential of germinal substance from which all self-consciousness is derived, is born into the viable substance of any A and B combination. Since it is impossible for man to have any but his own consciousness, he, C, which is every conscious individual, must die before he, the new combination of A and B, the individual consciousness which is the potential of self-consciousness of God in the germinal substance, can be born again. But actually, he, C, representing differences, is not born again in any sense of the word, simply because there is no relation whatsoever between himself now and someone in the future. You, the conscious perception of your individual characteristics, are you, no one else. It is you who perceives these individual differences between yourself and others, and you see these differences in the present moment, since there is no such thing as the past or future. Since you are conscious of your existence right at this very moment with all the millions of years behind and ahead (expressions only), and because there is no such thing as the past or future in reality since this is the perception of a fallacious relation, you, not your individual characteristics but your consciousness of these; you who are conscious right now of this universe, who are reading this book, have always been conscious simply because you, an attribute of God's self-consciousness, which continues from generation to generation in the potential of the protoplasmic substance, never die as you are the consciousness of existence. Consequently, any child born, once your body dies, is actually you nonetheless because the consciousness through which this new person sees the world, and the differences about himself, is always here during the present moment of time.

In summary, since there is no such thing as the past, and consciousness can only be your consciousness of this present moment of time, every child born represents the consciousness of his own individuality and existence. Therefore, no matter how many times you died in the uterine journey in the form of individual characteristics, your consciousness of yourself would have been born from any combination of A and B into viable substance. And whether you die in the uterine journey, at the age of ten, twenty, or one hundred years, does not alter the fact that immediately after death, any combination of A and B is your potential consciousness of your individual characteristics and existence. Because a mother and father become attached to the individual characteristics, which are you, it naturally hurts them to lose what they have grown to love; but if ten children died immediately upon birth, the eleventh child would still be you, who now becomes conscious of his or your differences.

The perception of these relations makes it obvious that the same general experiences we have gone through of being little boys and girls with a mother and father, growing up, getting married, raising a family, and remarking about the time way back in the olden days when man used to believe his will was free will continue throughout eternity because there is no such thing as a beginning and end since time, space, and consciousness are infinite and eternal attributes of the present.

If you stop to weigh the obvious fact that there is no such thing as the past (only now, the present), and this moment of time can only be perceived through your individual consciousness, never that of another, and that you, C, this ego or I you feel is not only a personal thing but pertains to the protoplasmic substance of this universe or God as an attribute of his self-consciousness which is carried along in the germinal substance A and B, the relation will soon dawn on you that consciousness, which is really not a personal characteristic, is the eternal window of God through which you, the individual attribute or ego of this all-pervasive consciousness which belongs to every living soul, looks out upon this magnificent universe in all its glory and mathematical harmony. Consequently, it should be obvious that God can have absolutely no existence unless through the consciousness of man, who is an eternal attribute of God. And once man fully realizes that he is the conscious expression of God who exists eternally because there is no such thing as the past or future, only the present, which is eternal, he will become conscious of his own eternal life; otherwise, he will be eternal unconsciously.

When someone dies, it is true that he is gone and will never return in our lifetime because these relations are also undeniable to our common sense. But I also know that my father and his father before him are derived from this protoplasmic substance that never dies and is handed along from generation to generation. It is very true that we have grown to love our fathers and mothers, husbands and wives, brothers and sisters, but their time of death and our relationship to them does not change reality. If my father had died during his uterine journey, does this mean that I would never have been born? Of course not, because the word I is a symbol of any individual that is derived from this germinal world of potential consciousness. This 'I' is given to us upon being born. Our perception that we are derived from two specific people doesn't alter the fact that our consciousness of these relations is not derived from them but from the inherent ability of man's brain to perceive these differences in relation, which ability is carried along in the germinal world of potential consciousness that imparts individuality upon being born. If I should die this instant, it only means that I, not the individual Seymour Lessans, but someone born of two new parents, would start my life over again because this consciousness of individuality is given to each person at birth and has nothing to do with the individual characteristics themselves. But it is impossible for me to have my consciousness and that of another; therefore, the differences that are now me must die before the new differences, containing the same consciousness as the child develops from birth during the present moment of time, can be born. Consequently, death is a mirage, and it is our ability to recognize these deeper relations that gives us our immortality, for then we know that even though God sweeps away our aging flesh, we will be born again and again and again. This is an actual reality, not a figment of the imagination, and can easily be verified when you realize that with all the millions of years, you, of all people, are born right now to see the universe. But you will also be born a million years hence because all we have is the present, and this universe can only be seen through your consciousness, not the consciousness of another. However, no one likes to die or lose a loved companion, but God's infinite wisdom, by revealing that will is not free and what this means, prevents in 90 percent of the cases any premature deaths by eliminating all war, crime, economic insecurity, jealousy, hate, and every other evil that was necessary up until now, while giving man the will, the freedom, and the intelligence to wipe away the other ten. In your Golden Age, the inception of which will take place very shortly, you will fall mutually in love, raise a family in complete health, security, wealth, and happiness, live to a ripe old age as we do on our planet, and die only to be born for the same happiness again and again. Is God a reality and is he good? You bet your life he is, and we are in wonderful hands!

It is because we know that God asks absolutely nothing of mankind since he directs us with his invariable law of satisfaction, which gives us no choice, that we are inclined to thank him from the bottom of our hearts for granting peace, understanding, and brotherly love at last.

Did you love *Inception of the Golden Age: A Scientific Discovery*? Then you should read *A New Earth*[1] by Seymour Lessans!

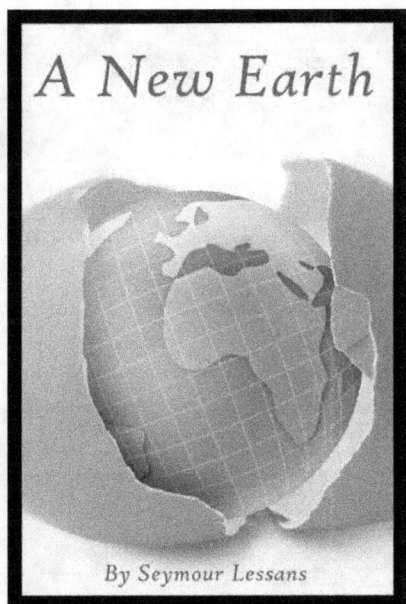

A New Earth

By Seymour Lessans [2]

A New Earth took five years to complete. It was the author's 3rdattempt to reveal a scientific discovery that has the power to preventwar, crime, discrimination, and many other evils plaguing mankind. This knowledge reveals that the long-awaited Messiah (the solutionto all our problems) is nothing other than a psychological law ofman's nature which has remained undiscovered, like atomic energy,until now. By discovering this well-concealed law and demonstratingits

1. https://books2read.com/u/4jPxM5

2. https://books2read.com/u/4jPxM5

power, a catalyst is introduced into human relations that compelsa fantastic change in the direction our nature has been traveling. Veryfew people, when first reading the Preface, which follows, willbelieve these changes possible. However, mathematical proof isundeniably established as the text is read and understood.

Read more at www.declineandfallofallevil.com.

Also by Seymour Lessans

Decline and Fall of All Evil
This Is An Urgent Message From A Visitor To Your Planet
Beyond the Framework of Modern Thought
The Secret
View From The Mountaintop
A New Earth
Inception of the Golden Age: A Scientific Discovery

Watch for more at www.declineandfallofallevil.com.

www.ingramcontent.com/pod-product-compliance
Lightning Source LLC
Chambersburg PA
CBHW072118270326
41931CB00010B/1599